Master
dating

52 brilliantideas

one good idea can change your life...

Master dating

Get the life and love you want

Lisa Helmanis

CAREFUL NOW
All's fair...
...in love and war, so while you may be playing the field and taking a few chances, we at Infinite Ideas wish you well but also remind you that we cannot take responsibility for any failed marriages, unsuitable men or bad kissers. Your choices and the outcome are down to you. We would, however, like to wish you well at putting these ideas into practice, tell you to polish up your date shoes and recommend a breath mint. Remember, anything can happen; hearts can get broken but also be mended, and no one ever won the big prize without running the race.

Get out there. You're gorgeous.

Copyright © The Infinite Ideas Company Limited, 2005

The right of Lisa Helmanis to be identified as the author of this book has been asserted in accordance with the Copyright, Designs and Patents Act 1988.

First published in 2005 by
The Infinite Ideas Company Limited
36 St Giles
Oxford
OX1 3LD
United Kingdom
www.infideas.com

A CIP catalogue record for this book is available from the British Library.

ISBN 1-904902-36-7

Brand and product names are trademarks or registered trademarks of their respective owners.

Designed and typeset by Baseline Arts Ltd, Oxford
Printed by TJ International, Cornwall

Brilliant ideas

OK, so dating doesn't necessarily mean getting frisky, but let's face it: at some point, it usually does.

Picture the scene: you are having lunch by yourself in a quiet café; you look up and see two men at nearby tables. Both are nice looking, of equal build, and both keeep looking at you...

Well, doesn't life just kick you in the teeth sometimes? You got what you wanted and you're still not happy.

It's a common complaint for men and women: but let's face it, mainly *about* women. You meet a guy, you have a couple of dates...

Die-hard romantics may want to look away now. Unless they really want to hook someone special...

Ugh. Is there anything more hideous? Anything that makes you feel more uncomfortable or loathe yourself quite like jealousy does?

Sometimes the wild and free land of singledom seems full of opportunity and wonder, with a veritable herd of possible lovers beating down your door.

Brilliant features

Each chapter of this book is designed to provide you with an inspirational idea that you can read quickly and put into practice straight away.

Throughout you'll find four features that will help you to get right to the heart of the idea:

- *Here's an idea for you* Take it on board and give it a go – right here, right now. Get an idea of how well you're doing so far.

- *Try another idea* If this idea looks like a life-changer then there's no time to lose. *Try another idea* will point you straight to a related tip to expand and enhance the first.

- *Defining ideas* Words of wisdom from masters and mistresses of the art, plus some interesting hangers-on.

- *How did it go?* If at first you do succeed, try to hide your amazement. If, on the other hand, you don't, then this is where you'll find a Q and A that highlights common problems and how to get over them.

Introduction

Who would have thought that something as simple and natural as meeting a partner would need a manual? After all, it's easy. Don't your eyes just meet across a crowded room, then you make idle chatter and impress each other with your witty repartee, and the next thing you know it's all mini-breaks and expensive dinners with flattering low lighting? Right?

Wrong. These times they are a-changing, and on an almost daily basis. Our expectations of love, romance and sex have altered massively since only a generation ago, when marriage was seen as a lifetime commitment and the most important one you could make. Now, statistics show that almost half of all marriages end in divorce and stepfamilies are a massive part of our social fabric, which can make everyone a little more jumpy about making another commitment and a lot more fearful of getting hurt again. Factor into this longer working hours, and the expensive cost of living, and – well, you get the picture. Romance gets moved to the back burner.

But the wonderful thing is that the heart is a rather resilient organ. And while there may be more divorcées out there (as well as those who have yet to make it legal), that also means more people available to meet who might, with any luck, be a little bit wiser. This book is written with this in mind: that your first outing onto the dating scene was probably the equivalent of fairground dodgem cars; bumping happily into each other, bouncing right off again if there was no real connection, feeling like there was another bump about to come right along. Then you hook up with someone for a while and ride the big wheel: on the way up it's all anticipation and the view from the top; you really have to see it to believe it. Then, before you know it, it's back down to earth with a bump and it's all over. Except it's ten years later. And you suddenly start to feel a bit woozy. Maybe the rides aren't so much fun: it's all roller coasters and hanging upside down, and you just aren't so sure any more. Things seem a lot more complicated than they were before. There seems to be a lot more to lose (like your lunch, for example).

Only the very stupid or the very thick-skinned wouldn't feel cautious. Meeting someone in the modern world has become notoriously difficult, despite the fact that there are more people on the planet than ever before – it's like we've all lost the art of making connections. Plus, the last time we were running around looking for a mate there seemed to be a lot more single people and it seemed to be a lot easier to meet them. When you are twenty-two, writing your number in biro on the back of a guy's arm while swaggering out of the night club with your mates might seem reasonable, but can you pull it off at thirty-four? And would he only call you to give you his dry-cleaning bill? There's a whole different art to successful dating as you get older: after all, you may only have demanded that your first love had his own skateboard, now you may expect him to own a skateboard company.

Plus, of course, there is the 'I can't meet a man' syndrome a lot of us girls hide behind. The reality is that almost half the population is male, so you need to accept that you are maybe in a rut, or just plain looking in all the wrong places. We will look at all the ways in which you can sharpen up your act, your attitude and your techniques, and give you back the control you forgot you always had. This will bring your love life back into the spotlight and get you central to being the star of your own show, rather than someone in an audience waiting for something to happen. (Has it started yet?)

This book is designed to help you understand any fears and motivations that may be holding you back, and bring that joy back from those early days when it was all a fun game. We've given you some special tools to use to help you re-enter the fray, like understanding the new rules (who pays, how do you speed date?), the insider tricks (how to know he wants you even before he opens his mouth, the ancient art of mirroring), and some good confidence boosters (make your own life sexy, keeping safe) to blast away any fears.

So lighten up and get reading and remember – anything can happen.

Enjoy the ride!

1

Where are you at?

The first thing you need to do when looking for romance is take a look at yourself. Not as a proposition, although at least you know you'd have something in common...

No, you need to have a long look at your life, behaviour, and even look into that sometimes unpleasant place, the past.

A classic whinge heard from most single women works along the lines of 'But I never meet anyone!' Erm, hello? Take a look around you: do you find your Saturday nights taken up by dinner parties with old college friends, sitting talking to their husbands and nursing their babies on your knee repeating the aforementioned phrase? Face facts. They are unlikely to suddenly produce a single, attractive man along with the dessert (unless they are using caterers). If you have met all their friends, colleagues and relations then what are you doing wasting your best dress on them? And if you haven't exhausted their potential supply, ask them clearly to rustle you up a possibility at the next dinner party – even if it is only a chance to talk to someone new and try out your new line in charming dialogue.

And when you do go out, do you spend your time with your back to the room cackling away with friends and bemoaning your ex, hardly glancing up at the man

Here's an idea for you...

Ask your friends where they think you are at. You may think you are ready for the love of your life, but find yourself faced with friends cackling like hyenas when you suggest it. Why? Well, you may be unaware that you drop your ex's name into every other sentence, or snarl at any interested parties if they as much as glance at you. And the reason you are unaware of this is that good, old-fashioned friend known as 'denial'. This is where your friends can help you understand where you are, what you are ready for and, maybe, what you need to change.

asking you if you have a light as you shoo him away? This may seem a relatively harmless way to spend your nights out – at least you are out of the house and in a public place, right? – but you may as well be sitting in a darkened room on your own with fifty cats. A recent Australian government study discovered that only 7% of communication is verbal, 38% is in the tone of voice and a staggering 55% is non-verbal (body language, to you and me). If you are serious about getting on the dating trail, you need to start speaking up with your mouth shut.

The reality is that you may *say* you want a relationship, but behaviour like that contradicts it. Of course you shouldn't stop having dinner with friends or just having a girlie night out, but you also need to make room in your life for romance. It is essential that you acknowledge that maybe fear, bad habits or just plain rustiness might be at work here. And once you know what you are dealing with, you can make a change.

So: ask yourself why you want to date – and if you're ready. If you are still smarting from the break-up of a long or difficult relationship then dating could be the great confidence booster you need, but it might be a good idea to accept

Take a look at IDEA 12, *Being lucky at getting lucky*, for some ideas on warming up your dating mojo.

Try another idea...

that you're most likely to need some time on your own before you are ready to launch into another serious affair. If you have been single for ages and think you may be covered in two inches of dust from sitting on the shelf for so long, you may need to a do a little 'kamikaze' dating (dating for the pure hell of it without a specified outcome), refamiliarising yourself with the process in time to make the right moves when the right one comes along. Or you may simply be ready for the love of your life, and want to start meeting a different kind of man to the string of losers you end up avoiding.

But whatever the reason for doing it, dating should be fun. You need to be prepared for some success, some failure and, hopefully, for some funny stories to tell at those dinner parties. If you are having real problems getting into the dating swing and feel nothing but dread at making these changes, then consider talking to a counsellor, life coach or even booking some flirting classes. Not everyone is born with Mae West's skill or Madonna's confidence.

But there's good news: like a sexy summer tan, you can fake them both.

'There is no remedy for love but to love more.'
HENRY DAVID THOREAU

Defining idea...

How did it go?

Q I want to date but I never meet anyone. What can I do?

A *Didn't we just talk about this?*

Q Yes, but in my case it's the truth. Now what?

A *In which case, you need to take a look at your bad dating habits. If you think you never meet anyone, it could be because you keep telling yourself that so loudly that you can't hear anyone asking you out.*

Q I am desperate to meet someone. Why would I do that?

A *Yes... a state which is on a par with 'My ex ran off with the window cleaner and now I am paying off his credit card bills' as an opening gambit for potential dates.*

Q Who told you?

A *Women's intuition. You may as well build a fortress of steel around yourself and take up macramé if you insist on talking about the past with anyone you hope might be the future. No one is going to ask you out on a date if they think you are still hung up on your last partner, unless they are a counsellor. And they will probably charge you by the hour for it. So do everyone a favour and cut out the middleman by seeing one man to begin with. That way you can let out your feelings, then go out and let your hair down.*

2

Who do you think they are?

As soon as girls are old enough to understand the spoken word, they are told stories of handsome knights and Prince Charming, encouraging them to daydream Mister Perfect from an early age.

Yeah, a great way to while away the hours of your youth but, ladies, don't be fooled. For grown-up women, this is the enemy of a sane and fulfilling adulthood.

That's not to say a woman shouldn't have standards. Standards are what keep us from ending up with the frog instead of the prince. But if you are serious about meeting someone, you need to forget your 'perfect' man nonsense and think more laterally about who you *both* are.

A great technique for understanding what you want is called visualisation. This means that you imagine yourself in a situation with your said partner and then note what is happening; it's a way of getting closer to your real desires. For example, in your fantasy, what are you doing? If you are laughing together, lying on a beach, that may tell you that you want someone you can relax with, maybe travel with, be

Here's an idea for you...

Tell everybody that you are looking to meet someone. This is also an important visualisation technique. Rather than saying you are desperate to hook up with the love of your life, explain that you are ready to meet someone lovely and have a nice time. It will make it more of a reality in your own mind and move it to the forefront of your life: it might also mean that your cousin suddenly considers the guy she knows at work as a possible date, which may never have occurred to her before. The more you put out there, the more you've got a chance of things coming back...

easy in their company. If it's a passionate clinch, it may be that sex and attraction takes precedence for you. Next, take a list and write down a 'wish list' of your ideal partner's qualities, aiming for around ten. You will probably find that you write bland things first, like 'a sense of humour', but try and be as specific as you can.

Then reread it. If you have written 'rich' but also 'loves walks in the country' are you being realistic? (Not that the two are mutually exclusive. After all, you could be talking walks around his *estate* in the country...) If you are looking for a dynamic businessman, then is it really sensible to imagine him devoting his time to hillwalking with you every weekend? It may be that he has to work long hours to be so successful, and you need to be prepared for that compromise. Otherwise, you are storing up a whole lot of misery for you both before you even meet...

What is most important to you? Would you prefer to accept security and appreciate the time you can spend together, or would you prefer lots of attention and fewer flash dinners? You could strike lucky and get both, but a little thought now could save you from ignoring your perfect guy because he doesn't seem to fit some very narrow criteria. By the same token, a little soul-searching may be needed. If you want someone free-spirited, are you willing to accept that you may have to share or even carry the more grown-up responsibilities of the relationship? If you'd love a playful 'lad', will you be prepared for the fact he may want to keep his Saturdays free for football matches with his mates? This isn't about making someone change but rather the opposite: being compatible after the first flush of lust is the key to staying happy, so rather than trying to force someone into an uncomfortable role later, be upfront early on. It will save a lot of heartache all round.

The best way to meet someone like-minded is to look in the places they are most likely to hide. For where to find them, see IDEA 3, *Where do you meet a straight single man in this place, anyway?*

Try another idea...

There is also an important thing to consider here: what the other person wants. If you meet someone that you like who hasn't shaken off their fairy-tale fantasies, unless you really do spend a lot of time in a pink ball gown and glass slippers, then consider walking away. How do you know? If he says he loves your high-powered consultancy job then complains that you don't iron his shirts (which makes him feel special), think carefully. If he leaps at the suggestion that you get a cleaner who can take the (washing) load off you both, then great. If he looks disappointed and questions your commitment – forget it. You may find that this request is just the beginning of a very long list entitled 'Hoops to jump through'.

'We come to love not by finding a perfect person, but by learning to see an imperfect person perfectly.'
ANONYMOUS

Defining idea...

How did it go? **Q** **I've met a lovely guy but he is just a bit old-fashioned. We have a great time when we get together but pretty soon we seem to end up arguing about politics, women's rights, who picks up the tab... Where do I go from here?**

A *Do you think if only you could change him on these issues he would be perfect?*

Q **Exactly! Now what?**

A *And if he thought the same about you, you would call him a completely patronising, sexist arse. Unless it is truly just sparky banter, then agree to disagree respectfully and move on.*

Q **Surely it's not so desperate?**

A *Not now, maybe, but if he wants a stay-at-home wife and you refuse to give up work you could be at loggerheads for a lot longer than you date. As the wise writer Antoine de Saint-Exupery said, 'Life has taught us that love does not consist in gazing at each other but in looking outward together in the same direction.'*

3

Where do you meet a straight, single man in this place, anyway?

You're ready to get out there and start mixing, but where exactly is 'there'?

First of all, you need to decide on your target audience and then partner up with some suitably well-briefed accomplices.

For example, a girlfriend recently devastated by her partner, who is looking for some one-on-one sisterly support, is not going to take kindly to you wandering off mid-groan as you catch some guy's eye. Try getting a couple of friends together, preferably in the same single boat, and head out. (Three is better than two, so at least you don't end up with one person sitting alone staring into her glass trying not to make eye contact with unsavoury characters. Unless she wants to, that is.)

Although bars aren't necessarily the best place to meet a mate, they are a great way of getting into the swing of things. (That's swing, not swinging: that's a whole different thing.) You can also have the benefit of a little Dutch courage although, remember, alcohol may calm your nerves, but may also affect your eyesight (beer

Here's an idea for you...

When you meet a person for the first time, be prepared to think how you can take this on to the next level. Met them playing tennis? Ask if they would mind practising with you some time.

goggles are called beer goggles for a reason). And as well as impaired sight, there is the issue of impaired judgement: make sure that you drink sensibly and don't put yourself in danger when playing about.

But you may have tried many a bar and club and found yourself turning away the same old losers. The key here is to break out of familiar patterns by trying something new. Offer to walk a neighbour's dog and pop down to the park when the five-a-side league is playing. The furry friend also comes under the heading of props – something which gives you and the other person something to strike up a conversation about easily. Other props can include taking up a beginners' class in a sport such as tennis or golf, where you are likely to be paired up into teams or expected to chat to other members of a team. If you like the way you look with wet hair, then get even more adventurous with surfing or diving. That way you can even take your new sport on holiday and meet a whole new set of potential partners. Just make sure it's something you feel comfortable with; if you aren't confident in a swimsuit, trying to catch someone's attention while you are snorkelling will feel like agony. (You might be more confident in an evening class where you can flirt in a polo neck.) If you are a film buff, try a local film club or see if your local arts centre has talks on cinema. It gives you the double benefit of a) the prop and b) a socially acceptable reason to start chatting to the person next to you, though remember to wait till the movie is over. You can also attend these events alone, which is ideal if you find yourself hiding from flirting by just talking to your mates.

There is also the category of chance meetings. Being ready to date means looking out for potential opportunities and being ready to act upon them whenever they arise. If you find yourself in the supermarket next to a handsome shopper with meals for one in his basket, be prepared to think fast, ask a question about the difference between clementines and tangerines, or just give a flirty smile.

Make sure you are sending out the right signals by reading IDEA 17, *Dress for success.*

Try another idea...

Of course, you can cut through any possible confusion (such as an actual explanation of the difference between clementines and tangerines) by choosing one of the more direct methods that have sprung up to service the singles scene. Personal ads, online dating, speed dating, dining clubs and matchmakers are all popular ways of taking control of your romantic situation. And in a world where it is generally acknowledged that it has become increasingly difficult to make time or opportunities for new connections, all of them are now without the stigma of 'desperate' attached to them. In fact, even the diehard romantic still waiting for the prince to rock up on his white steed could benefit from a few practice rounds.

An ideal way of easing yourself into the dating scene is to ask friends to set you up on a couple of blind dates. These come with an added element of safety (you at least have a recommendation through a friend or colleague), and give you an opportunity to shave your legs and put a good dress on: an essential part of getting on the dating trail. Plus you have the bonus of having someone in common that you can talk about.

'A very small degree of hope is sufficient to cause the birth of love.'
STENDHAL, French writer

Defining idea...

11

Q **I want to meet someone but the thought of doing something as contrived as borrowing a friend's dog makes me really uncomfortable. I want to find love in a natural way. Am I being unrealistic?**

A *But that's like saying you want to sit in your ivory tower until someone comes and breaks the door down. You are suffering from fairy-tale syndrome.*

Q **But surely some people just meet and fall in love?**

A *Of course, but you're not casting a magic spell here and manipulating someone against their will, you are merely increasing opportunities for the right person to happen to be in the same place as you at the same time. Life's a numbers game, so the more chances you create, the better your odds. Get on with it.*

4

Learn from the masters

Everyone knows someone who is an incredible flirt, whose social diary always seems to need extra fold-out sections and who seems to be adored by all men, from infants to grandfathers.

Rather than make a voodoo doll of her, watch and learn: the good and the bad.

BUT SHE'S SO *OBVIOUS!*

Most women with these skills often seem transparent to other women; they seem to turn on the charm unashamedly and suck up to a man's ego without a second thought. Well: newsflash – men don't care. And more often than not, they usually don't even notice that she does it to every other guy in the office unless she is known as the 'praying mantis' and eats her partners after sex. This is because most people could do with a little extra attention in their lives. Face it, even if you know the guy in accounts flirts with every woman he meets on the stairs, it still makes your day less dreary – and that's because flirting makes life more fun.

Flirting also doesn't have to be about sex. It can just be about remembering to look up, crack a smile and not take everything so seriously. You may not have just made a connection with the love of your life but it's good to remember to keep things light; it's a great way to stop every date you do have from seeming like a full-scale interview.

Here's an idea for you...

Look at the people who make you feel good and consider which of their qualities you like. Maybe your grandmother is a very calming person to be around because she is a great listener. Maybe your best friend is brilliant at coming up with exciting plans and making things happen. Your brother might always know how to put nervous people at ease... think about how you can adopt these easy ways of being, and look for similar traits in yourself.

RECOGNISING IT IN ACTION

Most good flirts have a few skills in common. Firstly, they smile a lot. That is not to say that they could be extras in *The Stepford Wives*. They just keep things upbeat, a quality that draws people whether they are friends or colleagues. Secondly, they ask questions and remember details; any good networker will tell you that this is an essential tool in making good contacts. It makes people feel appreciated, understood and special, so try and make a mental rule to ask more questions than you answer. Again, this will not turn you into some 50s housewife; it's as useful a skill in big business as it is in personal relationships. And thirdly, they often use physical contact, sometimes with themselves, and sometimes with others. Touching your hair or face gives the other person a clear signal that you are interested in them. Touching their arm or hand as you chat, taking their elbow as you go through a door – these are all ways of making people know that you are comfortable with the idea of being in their body space: or of having them in yours.

GETTING FLIRTING RIGHT FOR YOU

That isn't to say these are all right for you. If every time you see the arch-flirt you want to lock her in the stationery cupboard for pretending she can't work the photocopier when she used to work for Xerox, then you know you need to modify her tactics when you use them yourself. Maybe you can emulate the way she remembers everyone's name or gets involved with after-work activities (you might not fancy Bob in IT, but his brother could be pretty hot). It's about knowing that you might need to sharpen up your skills consciously without coming into work the next day with a completely different personality. You can use what she does wrong to help guide you: maybe her whole conversation is about the other person, which is a great way to get attention but isn't going to help move things on to the next stage. Maybe the neckline of her blouse ends around her waistband; also not a winner with every guy in town. The wise girl looks for lessons everywhere...

Find yourself short of something to say or giving a monologue? Read IDEA 6, *Too much information*, on how to pitch your conversation just right.

Try another idea...

WHAT COMES NATURALLY

This is why you also need to think about how you already put yourself out there. Are you always coming up with wisecracks or reminding men you meet how smart you are? Do you find yourself joking about, like you did with your male friends at college or your ex-boyfriend? Whilst this might be a great place to *get to* with a partner, it's not necessarily ideal when you first meet someone. Most people have a limit to how much they can take in during one sitting and definitely to how much they want to know. You may think chatting about your ex, your eating disorder and your PhD just shows your openness, but is it possible that you might be scaring people off by showing what a handful you are? Revealing yourself as you get to know one another is a much better way of allowing space for both of you to get comfortable.

'The mysterious is always attractive. People will always follow a veil.'
English writer and cleric BEDE JARRETT, from *The House of Gold*

Defining idea...

How did it go?

Q **I find the idea of flirting totally undignified. Surely if someone likes me they will make an effort without me having to jump through hoops?**

A *Ah, flirt phobic. No wonder you can't meet anyone.*

Q **Thanks very much. Maybe I just have my pride?**

A *Which is a poor duvet when the nights are long and lonely. Face it, your attitude is all wrong. You are seeing flirting as a desperate bid for attention rather than a little easy-going social oil that greases the wheels. Everyone needs encouragement, and a smile to a stranger doesn't mean you have to set up home, it just means you are approachable, should they want to approach. And if you find you have nothing interesting to say when he does turn up, you both got to feel attractive. So lighten up.*

5

E-love

It's a big part of our life and here to stay – the internet has revolutionised the way that we deal with all our relationships.

The benefits of cyberdating are obvious...

You can be clear about your intention for looking for a partner without having to be coy; you are in a free and open environment in which to flirt and chat. There are hundreds of sites dedicated to finding people with similar interests and desires. You also have a degree of anonymity, which may make you feel more confident. You can chat away until you feel like you know you have enough in common with someone before you make a plan to meet them. Advocates of internet dating claim that the focus is on the dialogue rather than the physical, so relationships have a chance to start on more meaningful criteria. For those who have been out of the dating loop for a while, it can simply be a way of re-entering the fray, in a much less confrontational way, while they rebuild their confidence.

The downsides, though, are pretty obvious too. You don't know if you are really talking to a solvent, attractive architect of thirty-three with no kids who lives only five miles away, or a bored housewife in Oslo. You could also spend so long plonked in front of your laptop that you forget how to chat to normal people, so just make sure it's a tool in your armoury rather than your reason for living.

Here's an idea for you...

There are lots of websites out there that are dedicated to art lovers, adventurers, single parents or same-sex relationships: almost anything, in fact. Try registering with a few different ones and with some of those which represent your interests closely. Some sites also offer dating evenings and get-togethers if you are uncertain about meeting prospective dates by yourself.

PAINTING A PICTURE

If you find yourself a bit of a blabberer on first dates, filling men in with every childhood disease before you even finish your pre-dinner drinks, then the internet offers you the chance to practise your editing skills. It's a great way to start thinking about your good points, about what you would like to project and which habits you need to break (apologising for your every move, for example). If it's not for you, say a polite thanks and move on. And if the worst comes to the worst and you can't get rid of someone, then that's what the delete button is for. But you could get carried away and post a picture of yourself taken at a time when you fitted those trousers you bought ten years ago and which are now in the back of your cupboard, kept as an act of optimism. The message here is clear: to attract someone interested in the real you, you have to be the real you, or you are setting yourself up for disaster before you begin. So be honest, and like any other type of dating, hope they are being honest too.

KEEPING SAFE IN CYBERSPACE

However, all the best wishes in the world won't save you from some very real dangers. You need to follow a few rules to keep you safe; if people are legitimate they will understand and respect your need to protect yourself, and will not push for anything that makes you feel uncomfortable.

- If you are awkward with the turn that any conversation takes, put an end to it quickly. It's not unreasonable or stuffy to expect people to keep it clean or friendly, if that's what you are comfortable with (but at the same time, if your flirty side comes out this can be a safe way to explore it – if you keep yourself safe and protected).

Want to try something with a more human (inter)face? Try **IDEA 3, Where do you meet a straight, single man in this place, anyway?***

Try another idea...

- Do not give your phone number, home or work address to people you don't know.

- Make a date in a public place and let your friends know where you are and what you're doing. You can even ask a friend to wait with you until your date arrives and have the two meet.

- Trust your instincts. If you don't feel comfortable, listen to that feeling and be prepared to end the date early.

- Even if the date is a success, consider the wisdom of allowing the person to give you a lift home, or of giving out your number. A little caution could save a lot of heartache down the line, and if they are right for you, then taking things slowly won't be a deal-breaker.

'Throw your dreams into space like a kite, and you do not know what it will bring back, a new life, a new friend, a new love, a new country.'
ANAIS NIN, novelist, from *The Diaries of Anaïs Nin*

Defining idea...

How did it go?

Q **I'm thinking of joining a dating website but am worried about people finding out and thinking I'm an undignified loser. Am I?**

A *This is the twenty-first century, and demands twenty-first-century methods. If you were living in medieval England you might have been taken to market by your father and swapped for a pig. Now that's undignified.*

Q **But what if I just attract nutters and freaks?**

A *That's the beauty of it. You are protected by the distance the net provides if you use it properly. And are you a nutter or a freak? Well, then. Lose your outdated attitudes and take a risk or two. Most people know of an internet romance success story, and you could be one just waiting to happen.*

6

Too much information

Women: we love to talk. It makes us society's social glue and brings people together.

The only problem is that there can be times, say when we have had the odd glass of wine or are nervous, that we develop a kind of verbal tic...

We decide that the best route to intimacy is an unadulterated, warts-and-all, four-hour narrative detailing our worst flaws and life low points. There are times when this is an appropriate route, of course. Like in therapy. But men frequently have problems paying attention to women that they have loved for years (like their mother), so a babbling woman they've just met sets off their warning systems.

GET THE ADVERTISING RIGHT

If you were selling a car, you wouldn't mention the time you spilled milk on the back seat or the fact that one of the air blowers seems permanently aimed at the roof. So you should accept that your achievements, rather than your failures (and without sounding like a boasting egomaniac), should take centre stage. But only

Here's an idea for you... Stop talking, and start listening. Call in the girls for support. Make an evening of it, getting in a bottle of wine and asking for an honesty amnesty. Give them free rein not only to mention your most cringe-worthy moments, such as the time you gave a two-hour monologue to that handsome man at a party about the time you got legally banned from going within 400 yards of your last boyfriend's house. Make a mental note to scratch it from your 'No, really, it's a funny story' list. Then ask them to list your best points, from your slim upper arms (get more short-sleeved clothes), to your great dance moves (add it to your seduction armoury). Write them down and stick them on your fridge; after all, we can be our worst critics, but can also be blind to our flaws – and our good points. Then make a conscious effort to make the latter a bigger part of your everyday life. It's all about accentuating the positive...

part of the time; it is a fact that most people – not just men, but definitely men – like to talk about themselves. If you find it difficult to come up with questions on the spur of the moment, then plan ahead. It might seem contrived but it's less agonising than watching dust and dead leaves blow through the restaurant during those yawning silences. It will also remind you to keep a check on your ranting; concentrate on listening rather than blathering.

QUESTIONS *NOT* TO ASK

There are some time-honoured questions that are guaranteed to strike fear into the hearts of all men.

■ The first of these has to be about his past, especially in the first few weeks of a relationship. After all, it's useful to know what's happened in someone's life, but if he is a disaster zone he will probably make that apparent through his own admissions, rather than through you probing him (such as a man who mentions his ex-girlfriend in every second sentence or blames every one of his exes for the ruination of their relationship). If he is a serious contender, the candid discussions you have at the beginning may come back to haunt you when you are more involved. You are also limiting where this can go; the past can tell you what has happened or can happen – but not what *will* happen.

Look at IDEA 17, *Dress for success*, for more ideas on non-verbal communication.

Try another idea...

- Next comes the mind-numbing 'What are you thinking?' If I could wipe one sentence from the planet it would be this one: this question is usually asked out of insecurity and demands – and usually gets – an untruthful answer. If he's thinking about breakfast or what's on TV you will be disappointed; if he is thinking about his ex-girlfriend you will be hysterical, if he says he is thinking about you, you won't believe him anyway. Do everyone a favour and pinch yourself every time the urge to ask this question arises.

- And asking where the relationship is going is like giving him the bus fare and handing him his coat. Of course, you are entitled to know what is happening between the two of you if it is not apparent, but do try and be more specific. The vagueness of the question is too much pressure, and most men will think that you are asking when you can expect to receive a diamond ring. If you actually want to find out if your relationship is exclusive then ask about *that*. But never on the first date...

'The opposite of talking isn't listening. The opposite of talking is waiting.'
FRAN LEBOWITZ, novelist

Defining idea...

How did it go?

Q **I think my naturally outgoing self is one of my best qualities; surely it's wrong to pretend to be someone else?**

A *There is outgoing and there is using someone as an audience. Do you find that you know nothing at all about a person after chatting to them for an evening?*

Q **Sometimes, but I can't help it if they aren't as quick. I get bored waiting. Is that bad?**

A *And do you always tell the same stories?*

Q **Well, the same funny ones. Still bad?**

A *Yes, stop it. It sounds like you are using these as a way to keep people at a distance. Wouldn't it be interesting to see what other people have to say, or would like to know? By controlling the flow of conversation you are controlling the flow of information: take a risk and try and let conversations be more mutual. You may be surprised at what you learn about others – and yourself.*

7

Love mechanic

Women are great at being loving and supportive. We can spend hours talking about the minutiae of our relationships, work traumas and outfit choices.

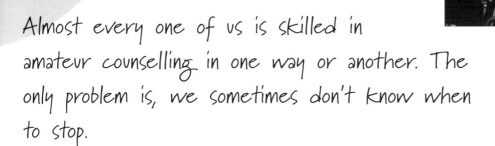

Almost every one of us is skilled in amateur counselling in one way or another. The only problem is, we sometimes don't know when to stop.

Sometimes you meet a guy who seems great. He's friendly and fun and so what if he occasionally accuses you of flirting with the waiter? You can understand that his ex-fiancée cheated on him and he will finally get over his little insecurities, right? Wrong. This is what's known as being a love mechanic, and you can guarantee that as soon as you have helped him work out his issues he will be packing his slightly lighter bags and moving on to the next girl: the one who doesn't remind him of his previous insecurities.

ARE YOU WEARING OVERALLS?

Sound familiar? Do you frequently find yourself helping someone out of a bad relationship or working through their past issues in your current one? This is

Here's an idea for you... **If you have tried shutting down discussions about the ex but they keep popping up again, then don't be afraid to ask outright how this guy feels about his past. Ask him if he thinks he really is ready to move on. It will either shock him into realising he has been inappropriate or make him face up to the fact he isn't in the right place; either way, it is better to know where you stand. No one wants to be someone's emotional mop...**

basically a pattern that *you* need to change; you may feel like you are being a caring, sharing sensitive kind of girl but until you draw the line, you will always be the one playing therapist.

SPOT YOUR OWN TRIGGERS

Do you find yourself frequently asking someone about their past, creating a free environment where they can tell you anything? It might seem like the reasonable thing to do, but it's not reasonable for you: if they have that much baggage they are more likely to need to see a professional counsellor than bend a friendly ear. People also have to want to move on from such behaviour; a man who refuses to buy dinner because he thinks his ex was a gold-digger isn't seeing you as a person in your own right, but rather as someone to whom he can express the anger that he can't express to her. In therapy terms this is called transference, where someone transfers feelings from one situation or relationship onto another – in reality it's called *boring*. (Sometimes it may be more deep-rooted, like someone who complains they can't keep a job because they lost their cat when they were five, rather than admitting that it's because they can't help stealing the entire contents of the stationery cupboard.)

Don't accept it. The best way to break such cycles of bad behaviour is to zone them as unacceptable. Looking away, making your face expressionless or literally changing the subject will let someone know very clearly that you are not keen to continue the discussion. It may be that they don't respond to this kind of tactic and persist, in which case you need to accept that they might not be ready to move on.

Take a look at **IDEA 32**, *Breaking up is hard to do*, for help cutting the wrong guys loose.

Try another idea...

On the other hand, we can all fall into bad habits and find ourselves doing things because we have always done them, not because there is a more meaningful charge underlying the gesture (such as spitting whenever anyone mentions an annoying old boss – it might seem funny, but someone watching might think it was sinister). If this is the case, you might be doing you both a favour by forcing a break from an unproductive cycle that the other person is unsure how to escape.

Final warning: if he talks about his ex as though she was made of sugar and floated down from heaven on a gossamer wing, get out of there. He is still in love with her and you are definitely a bed-warmer rather than a serious proposition. No one can compete with an idealised version of the past; you will always lose.

'The past is a foreign country; they do things differently there.'

L.P. HARTLEY, *The Go-Between*

Defining idea...

How did it go?

Q **I've met a guy that I really like but he seems to talk a lot about the past. I really think we have something between us but the constant references to his ex are starting to make me go a bit nuts. Am I being neurotic?**

A *Does he make her out to be perfect or poisonous?*

Q **She eroded his confidence a lot and slept with one of his friends: although he isn't mean, he needs a lot of reassurance. It's exhausting. What can I do?**

A *He can't judge the future by the past and once you have become more established these fears should evaporate. If you think you have a future then it will be worth the fight, as he obviously needs his confidence in women (generally) rebuilding too. It's not unrealistic to expect to get reassurance from your partner; however, make it clear to him that you are your own person and these are his demons. Whilst he may need to vent fears to expel them, you also need to agree that there are periods when you can have a 'time out' when you have heard enough or need to put the focus back on the two of you.*

Q **If that doesn't work?**

A *If there has been some abuse in his past relationship then it may be more appropriate for him to seek professional support to rebuild his self-esteem. You might have to leave him to his own devices to make that happen.*

8

Facing the facts

When it comes to romance, we all are masters in the art of deception – with others and with ourselves.

However, the key skill to learn when mastering the art of dating is the art of truth: when to use it sparingly, when to admit it and when to face it.

You will find yourself suffering unnecessarily during the whole dating process if you cannot face a few facts (and hide some). The first of which is that there will be some frogs to kiss along the way. And possibly some princes who think you are a frog. And maybe some princes who just aren't ready to meet the right princess, even though that might be you. And the sooner you learn how to take it on the chin, the easier it will be to move on and rejoin the dating fray – and the best side effect of this new-found resilience (bar saving yourself a few broken hearts) is that your plucky determination to keep on moving will make you all the more attractive to the right kind of guy. Rather than crumbling into a heap of Kleenex when a guy tells you he isn't sure where it's going, and begging him to tell you why all men hate you, give a light-hearted shrug and agree (even if you had already mentally picked out the curtains for your love nest). If he is simply testing you, he'll make the effort to get things back on track; if he really means it he has done you both a

Here's an idea for you...

If you can't make up your mind about someone, try writing it all down as a story, using other characters to play your parts. When we hear tales about other people, their mistakes or self-delusion seem obvious, but our own blind spots are impossible to see. Sometimes we try and make the facts fit our desires rather than facing up to them. Seeing things in black and white is often a good way of getting a more objective perspective.

favour by nipping it in the bud and letting you leave with your dignity to keep you warm.

THEY KNOW HOW TO USE A PHONE

It works like this: men and women do not operate on the same time system. Women multi-task; you can be filing a report, have a load of washing running, have a three-way conference call and still have space in your brain to know that it is twenty-nine hours and thirty-six minutes since he promised to call. This is girl time: every second counts. Men's brains work in a much more linear fashion. He may have enjoyed the date, then got home, then slept, then watched a match on TV, then eaten dinner, then had a busy day at work... and suddenly it is Wednesday when he finally decides to pick up the phone – and by now you are stuck to the ceiling with anxiety every time it rings. This is not to your detriment; this is boy time. There is a gap between the two, so learn to understand it to promote world peace.

Having said that, men also are quite easy to work out; any of the serious relationships I have had began with the man calling when he said he would (the next day). Men aren't that complex. If they want you, they will find you. Which brings us on to...

TOUGH LOVE

If it has taken him more than around five days to call, then one of the following statements is probably true:

- He isn't that into you, but wants some entertainment.

- He has a girlfriend and couldn't get to the phone till she went off to visit her mum.

- He thinks he is a player, and someone told him playing hard to get would drive you insane. (Note: this is also sometimes known as mental abuse.) He is incapable of/not ready for/frightened of a relationship.

- He genuinely lost your number and has had to track you down through Interpol, so desperate was he to see you.

Of course, you may feel the need to see him again to work out which one of the above is at play. And if it's any of them, bar Interpol, make sure you attend the date with running shoes on. Because if it is any of the above, you are better off facing a slightly unpleasant truth with a side order of disappointment, which may take a day to get over, than wait a few months down the line till your confidence and belief in men have both taken a beating.

Read IDEA 51, *Real confidence*, on why no relationship is better than any relationship.

Try another idea...

'*The advertisement is the most truthful part of a newspaper.*'
THOMAS JEFFERSON

Defining idea...

31

How did it go?

Q **Just as I am about to give up on this <u>certain suitor,</u> he calls me again. I have invited him to several group drinks but he is never available, but just as I forget him he texts or rings. What is *that* about?**

A *Well, you are basically his ego pump. No doubt he has no other romance on the horizon and likes to know that you are there, just in case.*

Q **But why do that if he isn't even trying to see me?**

A *Because it gives him a safe distance. If he meets someone and decides to drop you, he won't have to feel bad about himself because in his own mind he hasn't been leading you on. But, trust me, he's using you all the same.*

Q **So what should I do?**

A *Ignore his texts. He is a game player and you are getting nothing from this exchange but confusion, so block his number on your phone and start looking for a guy who thinks of you as more than just a prop for his weak self-image.*

9

If you meet this man, run

Some men are simply beyond saving. If you meet one and find yourself falling for his cute smile, try and imagine that there's only one space in the lifeboat: it's you or him.

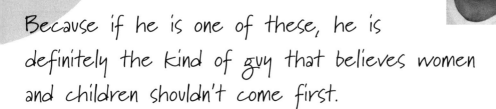

Because if he is one of these, he is definitely the kind of guy that believes women and children shouldn't come first.

HOW TO SPOT A 'DEFINITELY NOT'

Of course, we all have our off days, and sometimes we don't give the best impression. If you think that some of his dodgy behaviour could just be some dodgy, early-days glitches, then give yourself a time limit and hang in there for a little while. On the other hand, if he seems to fit any of these descriptions, if they seem to be a large part of his personality or a major pastime, walk on by.

- A man who has more beauty products than you do. There is nothing wrong with taking a pride in his appearance, but it shouldn't take up 50% of his salary.

- Someone who uses the calculator on his mobile phone to work out your share of the bill in a restaurant. Or an actual calculator.

Here's an idea for you... **Too many of these guys looking familiar? Had a run of 'definitely nots'? You need to take a serious look at the choices you are making and change your responses. Sit somewhere quiet and relaxing, then ask yourself what you did in response to their crappy behaviour (perhaps take it, possibly burst into tears). Now visualise a more pleasant outcome, one where you acted with dignity and expressed yourself well. See how nice it feels? Next time you find yourself in a similar situation, remember that feeling and act accordingly. It's easier than you think.**

■ A man that assumes it's OK to invite his friends along when you ask him to a friend's party, dinner, meet your parents...

■ A man who always complains that he is exhausted every night after work or whenever you ask him to do anything that involves your friends. This is selfishness of the worst kind: disguising his laziness as you being demanding.

■ Any man that says he loves you within the first week – it rarely counts for much if he doesn't know your second name.

■ Someone who turns being boyish into an art form. It's cute until he can't be relied upon to pay his share of the rent or leaves the baby on the bus.

■ A 'rarely available'. No one is *that* busy. A man who is not often available is usually not very interested or has got someone else.

■ Anyone in a relationship. If you genuinely believe that he is the one, then ask him to come back when he is free. If he is right, he will extract himself and come find you.

■ Your best friend's ex, father or current boyfriend.

- Anyone who leaves weeks between being in touch – to be frank, he is obviously looking for an, ahem, 'release' and you are it.

- Anyone you think would be perfect if you could just change that one little thing about them…

You'll find a few more tools to help you figure out his interest level at IDEA 11, *Is he interested?*

Try another idea…

ARE YOU FREE?

Sometimes people think they are looking for a relationship, when really they are looking for a way to fill their time, entertain themselves or get some sex and comfort. And there isn't necessarily anything wrong with those desires. Unless, of course, you are on the receiving end of them, hoping for more. You can, naturally, ask the other person straight out what they want, but they might not be honest with you or even be aware of their real motivations.

So you have to use a little common sense here and make a judgement call. A guy who wants to see you no more than two nights a week may be taking it slow or may just have no big plans for your future. Try upping the ante by asking clearly, in an adult way with no whining, for what you would like (three nights a week, perhaps). Don't explain or cajole; if he wants to keep you or please you he will think it through and reply, also in an adult way; if he wants things only on his terms he may try to make you feel like a demanding bunny-boiler (unless you are a demanding bunny-boiler, in which case get help). If so, it could be time to move on.

'Boys will be boys, and so will a lot of middle-aged men.'
KIN HUBBARD, cartoonist

Defining idea…

How did it go?

Q **I have a great time with the guy I've been seeing for a couple of months, and he always asks me when we can get together again and refers to me as his girlfriend. But when I tried to tell him about a work problem the other day he went quiet. Then next day he sent me an email saying he loves spending time with me but he can't deal with my problems as well as his own. I'm a bit confused. Well?**

A *Hmm, assuming you're not a terminal whinger, you are well within reason to expect him to talk to you about what is going on in your life. He is a perfect example of unavailable – he needs to accept that you are a three-dimensional human being and not a chorus girl. In which case, he needs to be prepared to help you through tough times as well as getting the laughs.*

Q **So where do I take it from here?**

A *Explain it to him clearly and see if he has just been thoughtless or a little freaked out (everyone does the three-month freak out; it's nature). If he insists he is being reasonable accept it gracefully and move on; he's looking for someone to fill the girlfriend box rather than a real, mutual relationship. You could always hang on in there; you may be willing to express yourself only with approved scripts.*

10

Doing it fast

The modern world moves quickly: and the perfect dating example of that is the speed-dating phenomenon.

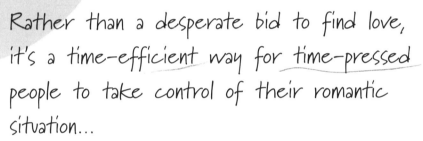

Rather than a desperate bid to find love, it's a time-efficient way for time-pressed people to take control of their romantic situation...

The advantages are obvious. You don't have to explain your agenda, break the ice or think of even making sure that there are any available, single men in the room (although, of course, there are no guarantees as with any other type of dating; you could be sitting opposite a married man with three kids, so keep your wits about you). But it is also a great way to get your flirting muscle primed: how often do you get the chance to talk to twenty-five single men in one evening?

SO HOW DOES IT WORK?

A group of singles looking to meet other available people attend an organised event at an agreed location at an agreed time. They sit at tables, usually facing each other, and follow a strict time schedule (there may even be whistles involved) of approximately seven-minute cycles. In that time, you are expected to chat away

Here's an idea for you... **Try going to these events on your own or with a casual friend; having your best friend at the next table could be a little inhibiting, especially if they are seeming to create more spark with the guy you just liked a lot. If you dread going alone, then take a casual friend from work or the gym that you know is single too. Make sure you don't sit next to each other and you can meet up at the end for a debrief; the natural distance between you will stop you from wrestling her to the floor and calling her a bitch if she gets a number you want.**

about yourselves and decide if there is any chemistry between you and if you would like to take it further. Different organisers have different rules; some won't allow you to discuss your occupations, salaries or age to encourage you to stay open-minded and ask more inventive questions. (You are also often not allowed to discuss more intimate details, either, such as addresses or surnames, in order to keep participants safe.) When the whistle is blown, you must move on and start again with the next person, even if you want to write 'mine' on the guy's forehead in lipstick. When the frenzy is over, you are handed an envelope with cards containing the names of the people interested in meeting up with you again, or you might just get the chance to mingle at a less frenzied pace.

MAKE THE MOST OF YOUR SEVEN MINUTES

So you have a limited time to impress, and you need to act fast. The first way to make an impression is to dress the part. You are likely to be behind a table so there's not a lot of use in wearing your micro-mini (slinging your legs over the back of your chair might create the wrong impression). Concentrate on making the most of your best features, and this includes subtly drawing attention to them. Make sure you maintain eye contact, smile and touch your face; these are all ways of making someone feel, and find you, attractive. Make sure your questions draw the other person out; you should be given some information to work with, so ask leading questions, rather than ones that can be answered with a simple yes or no. Pick up on things they say; if they tell you they love the outdoors ask them where they go, ask what it's like or for recommendations on places they would suggest. If you like someone, flirt but keep it clean; anything too fresh sounds desperate. And don't feel pressured to answer anything that you don't want to answer.

IDEA 6, *Too much information*, has great ideas for ensuring that you don't make the terminal mistake of giving away too much, too soon.

Try another idea...

If you do meet a guy that you don't click with, which is bound to happen at some point, then make sure you act with generosity. Be thoughtful and make that person feel comfortable; it's only a single-digit number of minutes and it would be ego-destroying to leave earlier, so make sure you have some stock questions, even if they are as simple as 'Do you have any brothers and sisters?'

A NEW SPIN ON SPEED

If that's a little too direct for you, there are now club nights specifically for singles which create an open environment for people to chat. You have your photograph on a big board with a pouch in which interested parties can leave their details. Check the web or local listings for events.

'The charms of a passing woman are usually in direct relation to the speed of her passing.'
MARCEL PROUST

Defining idea...

41

How did it go?

Q **I was thinking of going speed dating but I feel like I am going to clam up. I'm not sure I can sell myself in seven minutes. Can you help?**

A *You don't have to sell yourself, necessarily, especially if it means you're not representing yourself as you are. If you are shy, then make a joke of it and see how people respond. Not everyone is looking for a sex bomb.*

Q **But there will be a lot of competition, won't there?**

A *It's not a competition. This is a way to meet a lot of people in a short amount of time. That isn't about enticing people into your lair regardless of compatibility, it's about giving you the chance to meet more people that you might make a connection with. It's also about having fun. So don't stake your future happiness on it and enjoy yourself – at worst it's a lot of great practice.*

11

Is he interested?

Hurrah, you have found someone that you like. Now all you need to work out is if he likes you too.

If only he warmed up a bit... Well, relax. Reading those unspoken signals is easier than you'd think.

It might be that he isn't thinking about you in *that* way, but equally he might just be working out whether or not he wants to make a move and what kind of response he would get if he made it.

According to body-language experts, women have fifty-two moves with which to signal to a guy that they are interested; men only have about ten. Learning to read them is an invaluable way of working out if you are desirable to someone, and can take some of the agony out of second-guessing. Of course, some signs can have different meanings; touching your face can mean that you desire the person you are talking to, or it can mean that you are trying to work out what you think about them. This is, of course, because you have to work these expressions out in context, along with other signs such as eye contact and what they may be saying out loud. But it won't take long before you master the subtleties.

Here's an idea for you... **Try mirroring his actions, such as touching your face and hair in a similar way or taking up an approximation of his stance (unless he is standing with his crotch thrust forward, which might look a little strange). It's a good way of letting him know you are interested too. It sends out subconscious 'yes, please' vibes.**

If you want to make sure that you aren't going to crash and burn when you give him the go ahead to make a move, then look out for these signals.

■ *Here's looking at you, kid.* There are things a man does before he even knows he fancies you. He may lift an eyebrow, his mouth might be slightly open when he looks at you, he may stand apart from his crowd of mates so that he seems more inviting. He might not even have had a conscious sexy thought, yet, but it is heading to his brain.

■ *Va va groom.* He will start fiddling with his tie, pull up his socks or run his hands through his hair. All of these gestures are trying to get your attention, but are also a way of preening: yes, men do it too. Doing any of these repeatedly or all three? If he was a peacock you would be getting the full effect of his feathers by now.

■ *Check out my manliness.* Yep, even the most refined of men start acting all primal when it comes to getting what they want. He may sit with his legs open, giving you the full force of his crotch, place his hands on his chest or hips, or he may lean into your body space.

■ *Things speed up.* He may play with an ashtray, smoke more, drink more (don't we all?) or fiddle with his clothes. It's all about giving his hands something to do while his mind races through the possibilities of activities in which they would be otherwise better engaged.

■ *Gentlemanly behaviour alert.* So now you have finally got his attention, and he has moved into your orbit and may make a few of the following protective, ownership gestures which let you – and other men – know that he has an interest in you. This may involve sliding an arm around the back of your chair, getting you drinks or putting his jacket around your shoulders to keep you warm. This is the body-language equivalent of getting out his branding iron and putting his initials on your butt.

Take a look at IDEA 17, *Dress for success*, on how to learn to attract his attention in the first place.

Try another idea...

■ *Signs you can swing.* He may be indecisive about you, still trying to make up his mind, in which case you may have to work a little harder. Look out for him pulling or tugging at his ear (which means indecision), stroking his chin or putting his hand to his cheek (which means he is thinking about the situation).

And finally:

■ *Give up.* If he is doing any of the following things, you should probably give him a wide berth. Arms crossed means defensiveness, and rubbing his nose means he could be lying about something or rejecting you. Pinching the bridge of his nose is a sign of a negative evaluation and hands clasped behind his back means he is feeling aggressive or frustrated.

'Love is an irresistible desire to be irresistibly desired.'
ROBERT FROST, poet

Defining idea...

How did it go?

Q   I like a guy at work and I think he likes me, but will I blow it if I try and move it on to the next level? Don't men hate pushy women?

A   *Pushy, maybe; encouraging, no. Learning how to use and read body language is about letting people know how you feel without having to spell it out. You can actually find ways to let someone know that you are keen without taking out a huge advert in your local paper.*

Q   Like what?

A   *Good, old-fashioned eye contact. It's the best way of making someone feel desired. Recent studies show that people 'in love' hold eye contact a lot more than the average, and you can fake that sensation by making him think he's doing it of his own free will. Keep looking into his eyes and he will be unable to look away – unless you hold his eyes with the steely look of a murderer, that is. That would probably find him changing the lock to his front door for extra security.*

12

Being lucky at getting lucky

Got friends who seem to glide through life, people whom everyone calls 'born lucky', while nothing whatsoever seems to go your way?

Recent research has shown that there is a big difference between 'luck' and 'chance'. And you can work things out in your favour.

Chance covers things that happen to you without your input, like a hereditary illness or finding money on the street. But luck is something you can generate, by organising your life in a way that maximises every opportunity that comes along. So forget leaving your dating destiny to fate, and make sure that when good luck comes along the odds are already stacked in your favour.

RESET YOUR MIND

The first thing you need to do is change your perception of yourself as 'unlucky'. Most people can improve their chances by reprogramming their minds to think of themselves as fortunate; this means that you expect good things to happen to you and recognise opportunities as they come up, and it stops you from turning your back on chances because you believe things are too good to be true. The postman

'Reframing' is a technique often employed by psychotherapists to help clients get a more positive perspective. You place the experience in another frame which fits the 'facts' of the same concrete situation equally well or even better, and thereby changes its entire meaning. It sounds a bit complicated, but it isn't, so here's an example. If you had a bad relationship that has crushed your confidence, rather than thinking you can never get over it, try thinking that you are glad to have the bad experience behind you so that you can make a better choice next time. It may feel unnatural at first, but soon choosing a better way of seeing things will become second nature.

could be your perfect man but you might open the door without looking up every morning if you have decided that love is not going to come your way.

Start by resisting the temptation to relive your past failures and worries. It can dampen your spirits. Lucky people get things in perspective, look for ways to turn around disasters and expect that they will need to take chances to get what they would like out of life. When things do go right, even the little things such as finding a parking space, put that down to your skill: it will help you feel in control of your good fortune. If you find it hard to do, then jot them down on your calendar or on a notepad and see how quickly the good stuff adds up.

BECOME A SOCIAL BUTTERFLY

Research shows that lucky people have much wider social networks, and are good at meeting new people. So get friendly; at weddings, for example, be the first to ask everyone at your table their names and whether they are friends of the bride or groom – not only will you make connections but they'll all be grateful to you for breaking the ice. You can make this easier by looking lucky. Lucky people are optimists who expect good fortune, which radiates from

IDEA 51, *Real confidence*, will show you how to put yourself in the luckiest frame of mind.

Try another idea...

the way they carry themselves. If you don't do this naturally, then you can cheat: imitating their body language will fast track you to success. So avoid the folded arms, hunched shoulders, and lack of eye contact which ward people off. Be open, look up and around: how are you going to get lucky in love if you miss the opportunity to catch the eye of the handsome guy at the bar?

YOU KNOW YOU KNOW

Learning to trust your instincts will build your confidence and help you believe in your ability to choose what is right for you. You learn to move between 'hard knowing', which is the facts, and 'soft knowing', which is the feeling those facts give you, and you can then base your decisions on both. If you feel like something is right but can't decide, then write down the pros and cons and see if the result matches what you feel. Trying will also help you build confidence, because taking risks is essential to getting what you want. Still find it hard to take the leap? Try reading a few stars' autobiographies or watching films of their lives and see how many 'successful' people have struggled for years before getting their breaks, and also that life has ups, downs and then some more ups again. The one thing you can rely on, with luck, is that it will change.

'How can you say luck and chance are the same thing? Chance is the first step you take, luck is what comes afterwards.'
AMY TAN, US novelist

Defining idea...

How did it go?

Q **This all sounds great but I can't seem to get over the idea that I am a naturally unlucky person. What can I do?**

A *You have to loosen up and be prepared to look for the good.*

Q **But that's the problem, it feels really false. Now what?**

A *Of course it does, it's natural to resist change. If you find yourself holding back, worried about making a fool of yourself or messing up, create your own lucky mantra. Start and end the day by repeating a sentence that makes you feel positive, such as 'Things are going to go my way', or 'I can be successful in anything I try'. Soon it will filter into your subconscious and become part of the way you perceive yourself, and a natural part of how you interact with others.*

13

Keeping the boyfriend box clear

A big part of dating is being available. Yes, I know it sounds obvious...

But there are lots of ways in which you can say 'I'm free' whilst being utterly in the wrong place for having a relationship. Like the other side of the moon.

One of the great enemies of finding someone is already having someone, or something, in the 'boyfriend box'. This is basically the space in your life where your romance should fit and, wow, women are great at stuffing it full of everything from shoes to fantasy dream boys and not even realising it. Even if you think your substitutes are harmless, you are basically making yourself unavailable to possible partners. They might not be able to see the boyfriend box, but they can sense when it's full...

Here's an idea for you...

Take a good look at the relationships you have in your life and consider how you interact with each of them – if you have friends that you always find yourself huddled in a corner with, bitching about work, then they may not be the best people to also hit bars with. With those be a little more open, be clear that you do want to meet someone and would like to increase your chances. This might mean that you need to make some changes, like looking up occasionally, for example. If you trail round the same bars and see the same faces, then think about asking to visit new places or trying a new activity that will help you meet new people. That way you get to spend time with people you care about while still making an effort to meet someone.

WHAT'S IN THE BOX?

Well, we women are fabulous at keeping our lives full and rewarding. Research shows that single women are much better at creating support networks and involving themselves in rewarding social activities than their male counterparts. The only problem with this skill is that it sometimes means that between the gym, dinner with the girls and drinks after work you haven't got time to get out there and be in places where any new, single men might be. And sometimes people can be so concerned about having a blank space in their diaries that they don't make a space for chance. It's so full already, that unless you meet a two-foot tall man who is also three inches wide, he ain't getting in. If you haven't met anyone for a while, take time out to re-evaluate which aspects of your lifestyle are a vital part of nourishing you (massage treatments, your yoga class) and which could be dropped to make better use of your time (instead of women's singles what about joining a mixed doubles badminton club?).

HALF-BOYFRIENDS

Lots of us have someone who fits into this category and half-boyfriends can take many forms. It can be the 'maintenance shag' that you call up when you are bored and in need of a little no-strings hay tumble, or a gay husband figure who's your constant escort for weddings and parties and with whom you hole up in the corner and bitch about other guests' outfits rather than mixing. Pretty harmless stuff, it would seem, but they all take energy; the smart girl enjoys the attention and support but makes sure that these various 'partners' don't block her view from checking out those truly available single men.

So you are available and interested. Make sure he is too: check out IDEA 11, *Is he interested?*

Try another idea...

PAST STILL PRESENT

One of the key ways we all sabotage ourselves when looking to meet someone new is to keep the past present. By comparing everyone you meet with your ex, still reading his horoscope in the paper or mentioning him more than you use the word 'and', there's a chance that you aren't getting anyone new in the box because you haven't got room. You may truly feel that there is no one else in your life that you want more, or that you will never find someone you connect with as well as your ex, but the reality is that most relationships end for good reasons. There are no rules or 'normal' ways to grieve for the loss of a partnership, but if four years down the line you are still unable to let it go, consider seeing a counsellor. Sometimes we use a past relationship as an

'It is confidence in our bodies, minds and spirits that allows us to keep looking for new adventures, new directions to grow in, and new lessons to learn – which is what life is all about.'
OPRAH WINFREY, broadcaster

Defining idea...

excuse not to meet someone new because we are frightened of taking a risk, or are scared of things not working out and being in pain again. If you want to move your life forward, you need to make the commitment to it.

How did it go?

Q   I don't think that I do any of these things but I'm still not meeting anyone. I take care of myself, visit the gym and dress well, but I still feel invisible. What do you think?

A   *Perhaps you are finding comfort in the oldest friend of womankind: plastic. Do you shop every time you feel lonely?*

Q   Hmm. Well, I work hard and I think I deserve the odd pair of Jimmy Choos to reward myself. And it makes me feel more attractive and happier. What's wrong with that?

A   *It might help you feel more attractive but if you are getting your happiness fix from footwear, then you are filling the boyfriend box with stilettos. Accept that you would like to meet someone new and live with that feeling; it's nothing to be frightened of and will keep you focused on your goal.*

14

Putting the past where it belongs

Wouldn't it be great if, when you ended a relationship, you could just have it _wiped_ from your brain?

Or better still, if you could ship the ex and all his friends, family and even his local newsagent off to another land...

But, sadly, the reality is that the past can keep popping up with a sometimes monotonous regularity. That's OK; if you're lucky, talking to his self-obsessed best friend will actually serve to remind you of one of the reasons why you decided to cut him loose, as you give yourself a silent cheer while you walk away rather than humouring him, bored to tears. However, if you are unlucky, you might find the process of making a fresh start incredibly difficult, regardless of how much you want to make the change. There are some simple steps to saying goodbye, and do bear in mind that whether you are the dumper or the dumpee, you will probably have to allow yourself some recovery time.

Here's an idea for you... **Feeling flat or hurt? Try some human interaction without expectation, like a language group, a cooking class or even a white-water rafting class. It will stop you from just twittering on to your friends about him, and remind you that there are many people in the world that you have yet to meet. Make it a rule that you don't talk about him during this time; your brain needs some time off and it will help relieve your anxiety.**

FORGET FRIENDS

No matter how amicable your relationship was, or how calm the break-up, it's almost impossible to change the way that you interact with each other without some time apart. And even though you are sure that you won't end up falling into comfort ex-sex with him, you may find yourself using him as a comfort pretend boyfriend rather than stepping out and taking some risks with new people. And, remember, this way you may find yourself rethinking the whole break-up thing (which has usually happened for a good reason) and before you know it you'll lose the next two years to a ping-pong, back-forward, back-forward relationship that sucks the will to live from both of you.

FANTASY RELATIONSHIP

The great thing about the past is that it comes with free rose-tinted spectacles. As soon as the pain from the break-up recedes, you can guarantee that all the good times will start floating in front of your eyes like a montage of all the best Hollywood moments. You need to protect yourself from this illusory state by creating a list of your most miserable times, and his worst faults and most unpleasant habits. If needs be, stick this list on the fridge or put it in your wallet, ready to take it out when you are on the verge of buying a ticket to fantasy island.

And make sure you don't indulge in any 'what if...' or 'if only I had tried...' thoughts. Pinch yourself, tell yourself a firm 'no', or reach for the list – and soon you won't even have to read it.

Take a look at IDEA 5, *E-love*, on where to go to start some safe flexing of your romance muscles.

Try another idea...

DO THE 'RELATIONSHIP DEATH' DANCE

If you do keep thinking 'what if...' you may need to make the 'over' a bit more formal. This can take the form of writing your ex a letter expressing all your frustrations and sadness (but don't send it, repeat, don't send it). You could also invite your friends round and do a 'goodbye' ritual. This might involve getting a little fire going and burning a picture, or the aforementioned letter, and saying goodbye; it may seem a little foolish but it will help you concentrate on acknowledging the sadness, while underscoring the fact that it is well and truly over and that you can now move on.

CREATE AN INFORMATION AMNESTY

Don't ask mutual friends about him. Anything they can tell you will hurt: if he is seeing someone else you will assume he will marry her and it will make you feel awful, if he is looking sad you will think he is missing you and you will feel awful (worse still, you may be tempted to call). Make sure that you stay away from haunts where you might see him. If you don't, lots of sad feelings will come up and you may find yourself back where you started.

> *'What's gone and what's past help Should be past grief.'*
> WILLIAM SHAKESPEARE

Defining idea...

How did it go?

Q   When do you know that you have reached the point where you should start dating again?

A   *Usually when you can leave the house without sobbing and showing complete strangers pictures of your ex.*

Q   OK, only just got there. But I do find myself thinking of him when I am in the company of someone who might be a prospective date. How can I deal with this?

A   *That sounds pretty normal. Finding yourself in a situation that you would normally be in with your ex is bound to make you think of him. But you do need to make a conscious effort to put him behind you. Make sure that you tell yourself off and return your attention to the matter (or man) in hand.*

Q   But would I be using them?

A   *Transitional man or woman is a concept as old as time immemorial, and anyone getting involved with you might expect that you need to take it slow. As long as you treat this person with respect and don't mislead them, you can both enjoy a little ego-boosting fun and a pleasant distraction. Not everyone has to be Mr Right; some can be Mr Right Now.*

15

Dating warning signs

Sometimes when you are beginning to date after a break from the scene, it's hard to know what's right and what's downright wrong.

Of course, some experiences are down to personal boundaries; you may feel uncomfortable chatting about the past where someone else prides themself on their openness...

The good news is that you will quickly work out what you are comfortable with. But in the meantime, there are some clear no-nos that should have you shouting 'Cab!' Here are some personal hygiene and other respect basics.

Well, good hygiene is certainly a basic issue of respect; for you, as the date, but also for their own personal self-esteem. If your date arrives messily dressed, with bad breath and unwashed hair, then he may have found – to his horror – that the shower at the gym was broken after his pre-date workout. It may mean, however, that he is indifferent towards the date or a bit depressed; or basically that he's a lazy sod. If you want a project, have always wanted a career in nursing or have no sense

Here's an idea for you...

If you don't like someone's conduct, or if quite early on you realise that this little fishy is dead in the water with no chance in this lifetime of a second date, then it is acceptable to end the suffering for both of you early on. The key is to extract yourself with dignity, as there is no need to unnecessarily hurt anyone's feelings. If you have a dinner date planned, you can cut it short by missing out on starters or pudding, or if it's a casual drink, you can mention that you must go to a friend's birthday drinks party that you had forgotten. But whatever you do, don't torture both of you by getting a friend to call with a phantom 'emergency': you may as well just shout 'loser' at him in front of everyone he knows. Chances are, if it's not working for you it's probably not working for him, so if you think you can risk it, you might even be able to make a joke of it and say a friendly goodbye. Alternatively, if he is behaving like a rude, arrogant idiot, do whatever you want: a knock to his ego will be a favour to all women.

of smell then he may be the man for you. For the rest of you: get your coat, he hasn't pulled.

On the same theme, there are a few other fundamental behaviours that let you know that you are in the company of a gentleman. How the date is organised is often a good sign, such as him booking the restaurant or choosing a bar. Although lots of nice men don't take the initiative (and some who do are complete control freaks) it's a pleasant sign that he is taking the date seriously. Secondly, does he arrive on time? A man that leaves you sitting in a bar for half an hour might be trying to put you on edge; if he arrives without a genuine reason, then be wary. He might be trying to undermine you and make you feel nervous so that he has the upper hand. Although one missed bus doth not a sociopath make, make a mental note to notice it if he tries similar tricks as things progress. After all, it might seem exciting in the 'will he call, won't he call?' stage, but it will soon get tedious.

An age-old issue, that pops up between every couple at some point, is whether or not he (or you...) has a roving eye. It's not exactly polite to stare at other people, especially if they're not your date. A glance around a room is fine, but if you have to keep shuffling your chair into his eyeline, slip away whilst he's looking elsewhere. Five hours, the length of an average date evening, isn't a long time to expect someone to give you their gaze. And even if he thinks it's 'charming', it's not; this is not about being a playboy, it's about attention deficit disorder. He is likely to hit on your sister the first time you take him home. Or even your gran. Speaking of other women, you should also beware of any man who punctuates every other sentence with a spiteful tirade or sugary reference to his ex or, just as worryingly, his mother. Only general misogyny is a more unattractive quality, especially if he is asking you to apologise for the shockingly bad behaviour of all womankind.

Thinking of drinking through the pain? See IDEA 22, *Message in a bottle*, on why that's not a good one.

Try another idea...

A new way to offend, a by-product of our ever-changing, technically advanced world, comes in the guise of the mobile phone. It may be that he is trying to impress you by having several friends call or text him with jokey comments, or he may be unable to function without their constant approval. Either one shows a dramatic lack of maturity, so consider asking him to come back when he has got himself a spine.

'There's a great woman behind every idiot.'
JOHN LENNON

Defining idea...

61

How did it go?

Q **I was set up on a date with a guy that I quite liked, but he mentioned quite early in the evening how much he earns, which I felt was a little crass. Shall I bin him off?**

A *Telling you how much he earns might be a sign that he likes you and is a little nervous. What was the rest of the date like?*

Q **Great, he was lots of fun and seemed quite sensitive until that point. So now what?**

A *Trust your instincts. If he got everything right it might turn out that he is actually an android; if you are unsure then have a second date, what can it hurt? Warning signs should make you cautious but not closed; it's often a good rule to consider that if you don't know how to act, you probably haven't got all the information you need – yet.*

16

Blind dates

Blind dates are a great way to get back into the dating swing or give you a little perk up if you are in a dating lull.

Even if you aren't looking to hook up with someone permanently, it's a good way to remind yourself that there are interesting people about without having to do the whole pick-up scene.

Before you go off on a blind date, you might even like to try organising one, which will give you a good handle on how the whole thing works. It's a great way to get you into a new way of thinking, so don't write it off.

PLAYING CUPID

Taking a look at your male friends, the people that you haven't considered (ever or for a while), can help you see what you like in a guy, but if you're fixing up a blind date for someone else make sure you don't confuse your desires for those of your friends. Your predilection for nature-loving, woodsman types might not work for

Here's an idea for you...

If you think you have a great matchmake in mind, but one friend is totally reluctant to give it a go, you can always cheat. Either let the one who is up for it know the plan, or simply throw a dinner party or after-work drinks party where they can 'happen' to meet. Make sure you don't invite too many people, though, so that they end up not meeting at all and you have to start again – otherwise you may have to become a full-time host. And don't forget that some people are very private and would much rather not acknowledge the plan in public: you could always think of yourself as a stealth matchmaker.

your cocktail-loving, party girl mate. Having said that, don't just abandon the idea; make sure you ask what she really wants right now – she might be ready to hang up her slingbacks and get homely in a wood cabin. Don't make assumptions...

On the other hand, two people might look good together at first glance, but you need to think if they have similar goals and interests. A chatty crowd-pleaser might work great with someone who is more composed, so think compatibility and not just similarity. And do remember that two giant egos in one room could end in blood dripping from the walls. And, while we're on the subject, don't strong-arm a friend of your brother to take your newly heart-broken sister out on a date: you might end up crushing her confidence further if the phone doesn't ring twice. A good intention does not make a great romance.

HITTING THE PERFECT PITCH

See IDEA 18, *Recycling*, on taking some more dating risks.

Try another idea...

You think you have a good combination in mind, so how to proceed? Firstly, you need to get both parties interested and the key, here, is to make sure that you don't apply too much pressure. Don't tell your friend that the guy you want to fix her up with is the most gorgeous man you have met; she may wonder why you aren't interested or not have the same taste in lanky, boyish charmers that you do. Give the blind date a good build-up but keep it realistic to avoid disappointment. Also, don't fall into the 'too much information' trap; if it does work out, your in-depth description of his fumble behind the photocopier with the work experience girl at the office party (complete with photocopies) will come back to haunt you all...

ARE YOU BLIND?

If you're the one receiving the attentions of a nurturing matchmaker, make sure that you also keep within the boundaries of common decency. It's fine to ask for information such as his job, a vague recent romantic history (divorced, kids?), and an insight into why the matchmaker thinks you might be compatible. Make sure you have enough general background so that you can say something like 'Suzy says you're training for the marathon,' should things dry up over the main course. It will make him feel appreciated and warm. However, slipping in 'How's the treatment for the premature ejaculation going?' is probably a bridge too far.

'What is life but a series of inspired follies? The difficulty is to find them to do. Never lose a chance: it doesn't come every day.'
GEORGE BERNARD SHAW

Defining idea...

How did
it go?

Q **I went out on a blind date with my work friend's cousin. I think he likes me but I didn't feel any chemistry. I feel so unfeasibly awkward about having to tell her, how do I do it?**

A *You can think people will get on great, but nothing can predict that special X factor. If your friend has any experience in matchmaking, then she will accept that with good grace. Just make sure you deliver the news with equal elegance.*

Q **What does that mean, exactly?**

A *She took time out of her life to do something thoughtful for you, and must have thought that it would work (unless she was trying to just get him out of the house). So she might be disappointed too. Say thanks, then laugh it off and move.*

Q **What if she wants reasons?**

A *The whole matchmaking deal only works if people are willing to respect boundaries. If you loved his every fibre but the phone hasn't rung for three weeks, you have to have the good grace not to ply her with drink and beg her to sell you to him. At the same time, you're not a spare tyre, and she should accept that she can't pump you for information, unless she is willing to deliver the bad news. Plus, she might have another cousin...*

17

Dress for success

Clothing communicates, it's a simple fact. No matter how much we regard ourselves as able to look behind the façade, one of the first signifiers we read is the packaging.

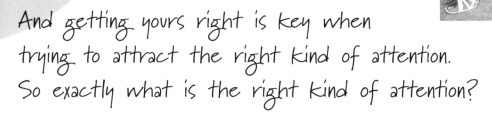

And getting yours right is key when trying to attract the right kind of attention. So exactly what is the right kind of attention?

Basically, you need to dress for the kind of man you want to appeal to, and for the kind of relationship you want to establish. Looking for a playful fling? As long as you aren't wearing a bin bag, it almost doesn't matter what you have on as you know what you want. Looking for a fellow art buff for a meaningful, life-long relationship? A spandex off-the-shoulder, thigh-skimming tube dress with some plastic wet-look boots may make other viewers at the private view think you are a performance artist. Or whatever. But you might at least earn your bus fare home.

WHAT HAPPENED TO SELF-RESPECT?

Dressing to attract a man might sound like the past hundred years of women's liberation never happened. But the fact is, wearing your favourite neck-to-ankle baggy jumper may make you feel secure but it does not, in any way whatsoever, say

Here's an idea for you... **Think about how your outfits are received; you may think you are being the belle of the ball but actually be coming on like a train. Consider the type of event you are going to and not just the impression you would like to make. A Halloween house party might be more suited to a fun homemade tramp outfit than an expensively hired catsuit; nothing says 'Look at me, I'm desperate!' like a bid to be super-sexy at all times. One quiet Saturday afternoon, try on lots of clothes and find something that is flattering, a little sexy and comfortable; then hang it on the back of the bedroom door as your SOS date outfit, if you get panicked. If in doubt, default to a little black dress. These have served womankind well for a very long time.**

that you are available or interested in taking things to a romantic level. Sexual attraction is an important part of finding a partner and there is nothing wrong with it: so get with the programme, have a good think about your best bits and pieces, and get them out.

FEELING FINE

So how do you get the balance between what you feel comfortable in and what you think might attract the right man? Firstly, you must feel comfortable in whatever you wear, as that will help radiate confidence and an ease with your body. And don't try anything frighteningly new or too high fashion; lots of men don't care that your shoes are the latest catwalk chic, but they might care if you take a head-first dive down the club steps because you haven't mastered the art of walking in them.

A LITTLE BIT OF WHAT YOU FANCY...

OK, you've got the outfit right, so check if it has had the desired effect, and on whom: read IDEA 11, *Is he interested?*

Try another idea...

It never hurts to advertise, and men are basically visual creatures, so a glimpse of a taut thigh, a crisp white shirt with a flattering neckline or a well-turned ankle in some killer heels are all great tools in your armoury. However, there is a fine line between being tantalising and being tarty. This is where the 'one or the other' rule comes into play. If you have a great décolletage, feel free to hoist your boobs up and dab some seductive scent in pertinent places. However, you may want to team that stunning, sparkly, low-cut top with some simple flattering black trousers, rather than a denim skirt the size of a belt. Even if you also have fabulous legs, too much of a good thing can slide into slut. So choose one good area and work it to its best advantage.

Now consider where you are going. A miniskirt with a black polo neck is a winning combination if you have devastating legs, but not if you have to hide all your assets under the table during dinner, with you now looking like a severe intellectual beatnik about to grill him on existentialism. The same miniskirt worn in the gods at the theatre might get the audience looking in the opposite direction from the stage. Be as objective as you can; you might love that skirt to bits, but if it's not going to work for you, put it back in the wardrobe.

'Put even the plainest woman into a beautiful dress and unconsciously she will try to live up to it.'
LADY DUFF GORDON, 20s fashion designer

Defining idea...

71

How did it go?

Q **I've got a first date with a guy that I met through work but I've very little to go on; I haven't even seen him out of a suit. What shall I wear?**

A *Ah, so you know he's interested, because you are on this date in the first place. But now you have the real stress of coming up with a winning fashion combination. In an information void, the best thing to do is pick your favourite outfit, one that you feel attractive in, and play it by ear.*

Q **But what if he's a rugger-bugger sweatshirt wearer, and hates my retro 70s cowgirl thing?**

A *If there's enough going on to think you can get through dinner together, then there should be enough to get you on to the next date. If you hate his outfit but think he's great you have two options – you can stop being so shallow, or you can get familiar with the boil-wash cycle on the washing machine. It was designed for weeding out bad jumpers in a non-confrontational manner.*

18

Recycling

You know the saying: one man's poison, etc., etc. You might find the thought of going out with someone else's ex a little unsavoury...

PLEASE RECYCLE

But think about it like this — we are all someone's ex.

There are some exes that might always just be a little too close for comfort, such as your sister's ex-husband or your ex-head teacher. However, you don't literally have to jump under a friend's cooling duvet. You can, however, ask your friends if they have any college mates, work colleagues or even childhood boyfriends that you might get along with. It's likely that you will at least have similar interests since you have the same taste in people, right?

WHEN IT'S OK

There are no hard and fast rules about how we find love. Some people marry their childhood sweetheart, some turn to their best friend at eighty and get hit by Cupid's arrow after sixty years of finding them as attractive as cottage cheese. (Bearing this in mind, getting involved with someone with whom you have a shared history, of sorts, can come with a particular set of problems. As a result, you should

Here's an idea for you... **Throw a recycling party. You ask your friends to bring along a man that they are not (or are no longer) interested in, and who is available. A great way to get the ball rolling, if people start lurking about in corners, is to give everyone name badges that they need to match up, such as superheroes or characters from books; that way people get to wander round asking other people if they might be Mr Darcy. If that seems like hard work (trying to work out who might suit who), then make it a bit more random by doing a 'lock and key' party. Get a set of padlocks, separate them from their keys and hang them both on ribbons. Your guests have to wander round chatting until they find their match. (The slightly sexual overtone – if you give the keys to boys and locks to girls – is a good way of frisking up the atmosphere.)**

think carefully before getting things going.) So there is no reason that your future can't be your friends' past.

GET IT OUT

The first step, when you know that romance may be on the cards, is to make sure that you behave with honesty and openness with anyone who may have to suffer the fallout. Change and transition, even when it can be years after the original event, can often throw up unresolved or confused feelings. If you talk to your mutual friend beforehand, you can take any feelings of deceit out of the equation. You may think you want to wait and make sure that you have something that may be going somewhere, but you might only end up making things worse. What would have been slightly awkward but easy to overcome in the early stages may suddenly seem like a huge betrayal. Inviting your friend to be part of your decision-making process might help them find it easier to accept.

You may, of course, find out that they are not happy for *you* to become happy with the person in question. At this point, you may need to decide who is more important to you: a new bloke or a friend who fought an embittered and unpleasant custody battle with him and finds it totally inappropriate that you would become close to him later (and she may be right). At the same time, a friend who is possessive over a harmless fling might be inappropriately needy. Work out if you are prepared to stand your ground if they hate the whole idea, and be clear about why. If you really think this person is the right match for you, you may have to say goodbye to your friend. Just try and work that out before you get involved. Tough call.

To find out if someone likes you, before you even get the ball rolling, take a look at IDEA 11, *Is he interested?*

Try another idea…

'We all have big changes in our lives that are more or less a second chance.'
HARRISON FORD, quoted in *Harrison Ford: Imperfect Hero* by Garry Jenkins

Defining idea…

How did it go? **Q** **I really like my friend's old college boyfriend and I think it's mutual. He's part of a bigger group of mates and whenever the group hooks up, we always seem to gravitate to each other. Do you think it's OK for us to go out?**

A *Unless she carries his picture in her wallet and has a shrine to him in her shoe closet, I'd say that was reasonable. You can always confide your feelings to her and see what she says. But be careful about prying too much; people are allowed to grow and change and her complaints that he never did the washing up when they all shared a house at university doesn't mean it would be like getting together with an adult version of the same thing ten years on.*

Q **What if she says no?**

A *Well, it's not a question of yes or no – unless she actually bought him in a slave market he's a free man. It's more a question of everyone being willing to work through awkward feelings and taking the time out to be sensitive, which can be difficult, but not impossible. She could surprise you and be thrilled; not every relationship ends with animosity or fear, and if she is friends with him now she must believe he has virtues too.*

19

Dating after divorce

There is a line from a song that goes, 'Nobody said it was easy, but no one ever said it would be this hard', which comes to mind here...

For a lot of people, dating after divorce feels more like a kind of slow water torture rather than a playful assault on a new life.

GETTING PRACTICAL

If only everyone who said 'You need to get back out there' was actually saying 'I'll babysit and I know a handsome doctor who loves divorcées'. It's not unusual for it to seem a total impossibility, if most of your social life was spent with your ex and all your friends are married – and if you have kids that's a whole other layer of concern on top. So, firstly, make sure you are comfortable with the time frame and pace that you choose for yourself. You don't need to be scrabbling in the back of the wardrobe for your little black dress whilst the coat hangers on his side are still swinging, regardless of others' opinions.

GENTLY DOES IT

Before you try and become the super-vamp overnight, you might want to consider less threatening human contact. A part-time job (if you haven't worked in a while)

Here's an idea for you... **If you find it hard to put the feeling about what you want into words, think of a character from a film or book that you are drawn to and try jotting down their qualities. It doesn't matter how vague the qualities are at first; just aim for at least thirty and pretty soon you will start getting into some interesting territory.**

could get you in the swing of talking to a whole range of people without expectations, get you coming up with chatty things to say and used to talking on a less intense, more easy-going level – the perfect pitch for dating. It may be more appropriate for you to have some counselling, do a class or take up a new sport, all of which are investments in your own self-confidence and esteem which will, after all, need a boost. If you don't address any negative feelings, you could find yourself blurting out some serious negative self-propaganda on a date such as 'I was so much thinner before the kids'. This sort of thing isn't pleasant for either of you to hear and will stop you feeling good about yourself. So every time you feel a negative thought start to form in your head, remind yourself of something good you have done instead.

THINK ABOUT SEX

You might, or you might not, feel sexual or be interested in having sex. But acknowledging that you are a sexual being with perfectly natural needs is a good way of avoiding getting your desires and your feelings mixed up. You might convince yourself that you find that hopeless blind date your friend came up with ideal boyfriend material because you are craving some intimacy and affection, rather than really wanting to get involved. Don't be worried about separating the two; it may stop you ending up in a nowhere relationship with the wrong man. It's your call about whether or not to get yourself a 'maintenance mate' (someone with whom you can take a tumble with no confusing strings attached), but you may at the very least want to take a trip to your local women-friendly sex shop and see what's on offer. You may find a new way to take care of yourself sexually and safely whilst you get ready for a new relationship. A sex toy can certainly help make your home life a bit happier even if it may not be able to help you with the washing up.

Take a look at IDEA 20, *Kids come too*, on how to deal with dating when children are involved.

Try another idea...

HAVEN'T WE MET BEFORE?

Well, you may be older and wiser, but all women are capable of returning to tired old patterns that just don't work when choosing a mate. A clever therapist once told me that people keep finding the same bad relationships/money problems/general disappointments because if you don't imagine what you want, you attract what you know. So you need to come up with a good idea of what you would like to find in your new partner. If you couldn't communicate with your ex, beware of following around the strong, silent type again. You have a much better chance of being happy if you look for a man who already possesses the qualities you want, rather than trying to shoehorn him into them later.

By the same token, don't just go for the opposite of your ex, which is a simple reaction to the hurt. Ideally, you should take some time to think through what kind of person you would like to attract, so you recognise him when you see him. The last time you thought this through was probably some years ago, with different priorities and without the benefit of experience.

'*Remarriage is an excellent test of just how amicable your divorce was.*'
MARGO KAUFMAN, US writer

Defining idea...

79

How did it go?

Q   **I tried to think of someone I find attractive but all I came up with was Brad Pitt! Am I shallow?**

A   *If so, then so are most women.*

Q   **I can't think of any reasons I like him. Well?**

A   *Which film did you like him in most?*

Q   ***Troy*. Where on earth do I go with that?**

A   *OK. Why?*

Q   **Because he played Achilles in the film, who loved war and wanted to be famous but was defeated protecting the woman he loved. He was strong and go-getting with the rest of the world but soft and loving with her. Does this help?**

A   *So you want someone who is willing to make sacrifices for you and put you at the centre of his world, who is dynamic but wants a stable home?*

Q   **Exactly. And?**

A   *Congratulations, you're not shallow. Although I'm sure it helps that Brad Pitt can pull off wearing a leather skirt.*

20

Kids come too

Should you even date at all? Well, everyone needs love, support and attention...

If you get out the sackcloth and give up the idea of a personal life in favour of pouring yourself into parenting, you may feel less guilty about the split. But guilt is a funny thing.

When you manage to bury guilt by denying yourself any time at all, you may find that as your kids grow up, it suddenly pops up in them. They may feel that they have to take care of you; they may feel that they cannot leave home or enjoy their freedom because they envisage you sitting all alone at home, after all you have sacrificed. And as we all know, guilt can soon turn into resentment. Does this seem a bit harsh? Probably, but as much as you need to reassure yourself that your children are loved and nurtured despite a split, you also have to show them – by example – that life goes on. By finding new friends, interests and even a partner, you are demonstrating to them that persevering is the best way to deal with hardship. Otherwise, you may well find yourself sitting at home wrapped in a shawl, damning their father's new wife fifteen years after the split – and you'll only be forty.

Here's an idea for you...

When planning to take things on to a physical level with your new partner, consider finding some neutral territory or a time when the kids are away at your partner's place. There needs to be a real basis for a relationship before the kids wake up with someone new sitting at the table.

I HAVE SOMETHING TO TELL YOU...

Some things in life are non-negotiable: the passing of time, ice cream *does* make you fat, you have got kids. If you meet a great guy it is totally acceptable if he finds the idea of dating a person with children difficult to come to terms with at first; after all, it does mean impromptu trips to Paris are out (unless it's in half-term and you can take in Disneyland too).

But it is never acceptable for you to pretend they don't exist. Definitely spend the beginning of a courtship dating as a couple before you introduce your kids, but don't try and gloss over how central they are, and will need to be. After all, if things move on, they will need to become central to his life too. By the same token, you can tell your kids you are dating but don't bring anyone home until you feel there may be some sort of future – unless you want to turn up at parents' night and have their teacher ask you about little Tony's many daddies. All your children need to know is that you are socialising and happy, and that's normal – not his phone number, kissing ability and that he hasn't called. Also, telling the ex is tough, especially if there is animosity between you, but it has to be done. There is no worse way to break the news of a new relationship to your old partner than through your children. The kids in question will know immediately, as soon as the words have left their mouths, that their other parent didn't know, and they'll feel awful about it.

I HATE YOU!

Take a look at IDEA 44, *Live sexy*, on how to get yourself in the right frame of mind for finding the man you want.

Try another idea...

Oh, that loving refrain that every child utters to a parent at some or, more often, several stages in their life. If you have met someone you like and are ready to take them home, then be prepared for some negative fallout. Kids will fear any big change, especially if they have been through one relatively recently, and feel a loyalty to the absent parent. Even teenagers can harbour fantasies about their parents reuniting, so give them some room. And if your date is sensible, he should expect this too. Having said that, maybe you should draw the line at your kids trying to lock him out of the house.

MEET THE LITTLE MONSTERS

When is the right time? Just because you are a bit older it doesn't mean that you're immune to a crush, especially if you have felt neglected or bruised by your break-up. So try and avoid that early, three-month stage where even your new amour's yawns seem cute; you may just be wanting it to work out rather than seeing it for what it is. And when you do know it's more than just your hormones talking, meet away from the home so the kids don't feel invaded. If your date has kids, let them come into the picture later; too much at one time could spin them all into orbit. They might panic at the thought of having to share their bedrooms with any step-siblings, and be closed off to the whole idea.

Even before they get out of the car. You may see wonderful adult character traits in your new partner that your children don't understand: be patient.

'When I meet a man I ask myself, "Is this the man I want my children to spend their weekends with?"'
RITA RUDNER, US comedian

Defining idea...

83

Q I want to date but I feel that the kids need me around right now. How can I meet someone and keep my children happy?

A *If you feel, therefore, that going to bars is not right for you, why not try taking them to a theatre group where you might find other single parents to chat to, where the kids are occupied and your eye can rove?*

Q Good idea, but I worry that everyone else will be married. Now what?

A *Then look in your local paper for single-parent groups. There are also companies that specialise in single-parent family holidays – all ways of meeting other people whom you can share your concerns with, as well as a nice cocktail after the kids are in bed. At the very least it will remind you that you are in a common situation and you can return with a slimming tan and, hopefully, the confidence to get out there and hit those bars.*

21

Why men love bitches

We've all met them; they are part of our daily lives and always will be.

And we've all looked at the bitch with the nice guy hanging on her every word and felt utterly perplexed and despondent at their union. What on earth does he see in her?

A more useful question to you would be what *you* don't.

GOOD BITCH AND BAD BITCH

The first step here is to identify what a bitch actually is. Of course, in technical terms it is a female dog, but in the context of its application to the female of the human species, it tends to depend on who's saying it. If a woman says it about another woman, it usually means she is tough, hard or cruel; if a man says it, it usually means he hasn't got his way. The second is probably the kind of woman that I would say falls into the 'good' bitch school, and we could all probably take a few lessons from her.

Here's an idea for you... Try saying no in all kinds of situations and see how it feels. Asked to do overtime you don't want to do or babysit a friend's kids? Say no with a smile and don't be tempted to explain – it's a favour they are requiring, not something you have to justify not doing. Be prepared for people to be angry or unreasonable, but remind yourself that those are their emotions and not yours. Once you get into the swing of drawing up boundaries you'll find it easier to stand your ground with a man you really like.

NICE GIRLS COME LAST

The problem with us girls, is that from the word go we are brought up to believe that compromising, putting others first and being amiable will be the key to popularity and appreciation. Fast forward about twenty-five years to kitchen tables and listen to the repeated refrain of women telling their best friends, 'I'm so taken for granted, he treats me like his mother!'. Well, that's because you act like it. Men are simple creatures; if you wash his socks, cook his meals and nod passively at his boring stories it's not going to take too long before he confuses the two of you. This is where the bitch factor comes in: the bitch will do these things but will also make sure – as her partner would – that it takes effort and that she expects appreciation, and maybe the odd Tiffany's box, in exchange for doing them. It's a rare breed of man indeed that does this without being reminded.

TELL HIM STRAIGHT

The key quality a bitch needs to adopt in practice is the ability to say no. If you don't want to do something, don't go and do it and then seethe in quiet resentment. It makes you feel uncomfortable and him want to avoid you like the plague. So just get it out. One of the best things I ever did in my dating history was stand up for myself. I decided to tell a beau who hadn't commented on my

splendid outfit all night that I thought he was
rude. He replied that he didn't do
compliments. So I told him it was essential to
my sense of attractiveness that the man I was
dating complimented me, and perhaps rather

Look at IDEA 51, *Real confidence*, on how making yourself happy first helps you say no.

Try
another
idea...

than make each other miserable trying to get things from each other we didn't
want to give, we should shake hands and move on. He had a little think about it,
and on date two commented on how great I looked within the first ten minutes;
from then on he was a veritable chatterbox on the feel-good front. He found he
enjoyed expressing himself happily and I felt totally appreciated. The basic rule here
being that you get what you ask for.

HIGH MAINTENANCE

Something many women fear is being regarded as high maintenance – but does
anyone really want to be regarded as low maintenance? If you act like you only
need the scraps from a man's emotional table, you can't really blame him for not
giving you a feast. It's not his job to second-guess you. If you are clear about your
needs and communicate them in a pleasant, unemotional way you stand a better
chance of getting what you want. Saying 'Seven is too early to meet this evening for
me, eight is better,' will let him know that you have a life and are not so desperate
for attention that you will drop everything for his. You might see missing your
lunch hour so you can finish your work early
and make the date on time as being helpful,
but he will see it as being needy. And the more
he pulls away the more tempting it is to try and
please him. Not a great power balance to set up
in the early days.

'The thing women have got to
learn is that nobody gives
you power. You just take it.'
ROSEANNE BARR, US comedian and
actress

Defining
idea...

87

How did it go?

Q **I really like this guy but your new rules suggest I should hold back; isn't that a bit manipulative?**

A *Did you ever date a man you liked but who was just that bit too keen?*

Q **Of course. So what?**

A *And didn't you wish he could just hold it all together a bit more, as you got bored and your eye wandered?*

Q **Yep, I felt smothered even though he was a great guy. Why?**

A *That's because desire needs space to grow, and if you are too available to him all the time there's no challenge. We all want to look at our partners and feel like we have won the prize. Not like we are doing them a favour.*

22

Message in a bottle

Alcohol, the great lifter of spirits, calmer of nerves and friend of the good times. If only that was all it did...

Because while it has its virtues, it can also cause a whole big heap of trouble.

Alcohol affects the part of the brain that deals with inhibition, which won't surprise anyone who has found themselves on top of a table shaking their booty in only a pair of wellies and a badly fitting nurse's outfit on New Year's Eve (just me, then?). So while alcohol may make it possible for you to say a full sentence without stuttering when you're on a date, it may also mean that the sentence is a rather intimate list of all the embarrassing men you've ever slept with. Might seem funny at the time, less so when the dawn approaches and the vodka and tonic wears off. And remember, 55% of communication is non-verbal so think of all the subtleties you'll miss if you are hammered the whole time.

WHERE AM I?

It's easy to forget that you are on a date rather than out with the girls; while you may think nothing of polishing off a couple of bottles between you and your mates and dancing the night away, it's not necessarily the way forward with a new man. Remember, you need to be thinking and chatting, and considering this person; you

Here's an idea for you... If you are unsure about a potential date, suggest something that doesn't involve night-time pursuits and see how you get on. A trip to an art gallery or a stroll through a park will let you see how you interact without the glamour an evening date can create; you may have a flirty thing going on in a darkened bar but be unable to sustain a daytime chat. If it's right, then you will get the chance to find out some more personal things about each other. (And you'll make sure you still fancy him in daylight.)

don't know him or his interests so dragging him up to the bar for a tequila slammer might seem playful to you but a bit unnerving to him.

There probably isn't a woman in the land who hasn't woken up with a fuzzy head in the bed of someone they wouldn't have chosen as their dream lover if they hadn't had that last Long Island Iced Tea. Although it might not be the end of the world, it doesn't tend to do a lot for the self-esteem either, so you could always cut out the middleman (literally) and avoid having to do the walk of shame home the next day, with your mascara down your cheeks and your ego in your handbag. When you start to feel like your judgement is going, get a cab. If you like each other you can get together again; if not you will be glad you woke up in your own bed (alone). And if it is just some nice casual maintenance sex you are after, wouldn't it be better to be able to remember it?

EASY, TIGER

Look at IDEA 23, *Smart dating*, on how to keep safe while dating.

Try another idea...

There are a few great tricks to make sure that you don't end up drinking yourself into a stupor on your date. Firstly, make sure that you order water as well as wine with dinner and take alternate sips. This will help with your hangover as well as your clarity. Secondly, if you are meeting for cocktails, resist the urge to order a martini and go for something a little more sedate; a longer drink, mixed with fruit juice or soda, can pack a punch but also keep you this side of bursting into Cole Porter classics. If you are going speed-dating or to a party, then make sure that you don't arrive too early, otherwise you are bound to start drinking to calm your nerves.

ANOTHER GLASS, MY DEAR?

Safety is an issue you can't ignore. In the first place, the more you drink, the more risks you take. Secondly, if your date seems intent on filling your glass, alarm bells should be ringing. Of course, he may just be trying to keep things convivial but the phrase 'Are you trying to get me drunk?' is a cliché for a reason. Make sure that you pace yourself despite his efforts. He may not be trying to get you into bed, of course; he may just be an alcoholic. Either way, you've got to wonder if he's second-date material.

'One reason I don't drink is that I want to know when I am having a good time.'
NANCY ASTOR, politician and first woman MP in Britain

Defining idea...

How did
it go?

Q   Isn't not drinking just giving in to the idea that women should be well behaved and sweet? I am a party girl and think I would be better off being myself.

A   But surely you wouldn't go to a job interview or a funeral drunk?

Q   Wow, you make dating sound like real fun. Is it, like that?

A   It is, if you get it right. After all, if your date turned up for dinner dressed in a sweaty gym outfit and chewing gum you would feel disrespected, and that he was being really inappropriate. And no one said stop drinking, just rein it in on your first few meetings.

Q   So when *do* I get to let my hair down?

A   Save your crazy nights for your friends and not your date until you get to know each other better, then go partying together; otherwise you are just forcing him to dance to your tune before you even know what he's about.

23

Smart dating

Dating is great. It's fun, liberating and can make you feel wonderfully alive and attractive. But, like anything, you've got to be sensible about it too.

To make sure that you can relax and have a great time, you can take some really easy steps to protect yourself.

This is not designed to unduly worry you, but as my mother (and everyone else's) always used to say, 'Better to be safe than sorry'. After all, the handsome stranger at the bar is just that: a stranger.

GETTING TO KNOW YOU...

Here are some things you should think about.

- Make sure you know all the basics about the guy; if you meet in a bar, make sure you know where he works (also a good way of checking that he has a job), where he lives and his last name. Sounds ridiculous, but it's not unheard of to find yourself on a date and be too embarrassed to ask his surname. Now, this is a bit unfair, but when asked the same questions be vague: let him know what you do

Always trust your intuition, it's there for a reason. If you feel uneasy on a date, get yourself out of there; a good guy will respect your rights to feel safe. And a funny reaction from a bad guy is a really good shortcut to knowing that he is not for you.

and the area you work in, the area you live in but not the street. When arranging the date, give out your mobile phone number; that way you can have his calls blocked should you need to.

- Make sure that your first date is somewhere neutral, not your local pub. For two reasons: one, you may not like him and not want to see him turn up in your favourite watering hole asking when you're next free; two, it's likely to be near your home so you may have a few drinks and end up inviting him back just because it's so close. Choose somewhere busy and easy to get to so you aren't stranded at the end of the date. When you are in a bar, make contact in some way with the bartender or waiter so they will remember you, like having a joke or by ordering a yard of ale (my joke, but find something distinctive to do).

- Let your date know that you have talked about him and your meeting, and make sure you do this. Let a friend know where you are and what you have planned. It's an old trick, but you could even get one to call your mobile – at the very least, you look popular!

- Transport is also a key issue. Don't let the date pick you up from home or share a cab home with you. (And, as you would on any normal night, make sure it is a registered cab.)

- Don't leave your drink on the bar; the use of date rape drugs is on the increase, so be alert (it's not just your date who would have access to it). The same with your handbag; don't leave your bag about as it will have your keys, your address, maybe your diary… all manner of personal information in it that you are unlikely to want to share.

- Go Dutch by paying half the bill if you suspect it's a one-off date; that way you won't feel under any obligation to return the favour. Even if you think you may see him again, don't let him pay if you feel uncomfortable.

- Keep your wits about you. You can be laughing, have great chemistry and feel like something special might be happening, but five hours usually isn't quite long enough to work out exactly who he is. Some charmers specialise in saying all the right things for all the wrong reasons.

- For the super-paranoid, there are some great ways to make sure that you are like the Pentagon… Have a separate email account for dates so you don't ever have to reply if you don't want to, and make your phone number unlisted, blocking your caller ID number using your phone company's service. Both ideas are especially useful if you are engaging in a lot of internet dating.

Take a look at IDEA 22, *Message in a bottle*, on how to drink sensibly when dating a new man.

Try another idea...

'If you wish to succeed in life, make perseverance your bosom friend, experience your wise counsellor, caution your elder brother, and hope your guardian is genius.'
JOSEPH ADDISON, English essayist, poet and politician

Defining idea...

95

How did it go?

Q **I went on a date and put all this into practice but I just felt as if I was an uptight prig. Surely there should be a little more lightness to dating than this? I may as well hand him a questionnaire and frisk him at the door for weapons.**

A *That might possibly give him the wrong idea. Listen, practically every guy you come across will be normal and nice, but not everyone is lovely and the bad guys don't usually have horns and a tail to mark them out from the rest.*

Q **But won't I just look like a crazy, neurotic person – not exactly a turn on, is it?**

A *And neither is a woman so desperate for a date that she puts her safety last.*

Q **That's not very nice. Surely there's a middle ground?**

A *Not between safe and unsafe: it's pretty much black and white. It's only making you feel uneasy because it seems false and contrived; once you have practised safe dating a few times you will quickly become accustomed to these measures, and they'll become second nature. If you feel stupid, consider what advice you would give to a younger sister or niece, and take it yourself.*

24

The big freeze

Sometimes things just don't work out. You can have a great time for three months and think it's all going fantastically...

But before you know it, things don't feel right and there seem to be more sad times than glad.

When you ask him what's wrong, he says nothing and gives you a pat on the knee. Grab your coat and get out of there; this is a man digging an escape tunnel.

So why do we women persist in a relationship that has stopped being satisfying? Because we choose to listen to what he is saying with his mouth and not with his actions. It would be wonderful if men simply said, 'This isn't working for me any more, but thanks for the good times and I hope you are happy.' But, in reality, they are much more likely to freeze a woman out and hope she pulls the plug, rather than do the nasty work of ending the relationship themselves. The problem is, us girls can hang in for the grim death, imagining that we can make things better, trying even harder to please. So, while he is waiting for you to make your exit, he gets regular sex, an extra-attentive lady and the comfort of having someone around. And your self-esteem gets to slide down the drain.

Here's an idea for you...

You may think that your relationship is just going through a bad patch, which might be true. If you start to recognise warning signals you could always calmly ask if the other person wants to end things (although don't ask this every other day; it sort of loses its edge). They might surprise you with a clear 'yes', or it could open up a discussion which would clear the air. But you also have to ask yourself if you want to be in a relationship based on these kinds of exchanges.

WAKEY, WAKEY

The best way to handle a man on the move is to let him go. You might think everything is lovely but if he just isn't into it, what's the point in trying to persuade him? He will only try and make a run for it at some later point, probably when you have more invested in the relationship and find it even harder to let go. You won't always be able to find out what the reason is for someone leaving: they may not be over their ex, maybe they want to focus on work or are just not feeling it. What you can control, however, is your response. While it is fine to be upset and feel a bit rejected (it's only natural, after all), there is no point in trying to jump through hoops persuading him you are the right girl for him unless you are prepared to keep it up for the next sixty years. I call this urge to please the 'blue hat on a Tuesday' syndrome. Basically, it covers the 'if only I was thinner/blonder/ smarter/sportier' statements that mean about as much as 'if only I had worn a blue hat on a Tuesday'. If you are not the right woman, then trying to do an impression of the right woman is not going to convince him. Good relationships allow both partners to change because the important thing stays constant – that they are the person that the other wants to be with.

WARNING SIGNS THAT HE IS OUT THE DOOR

There are some real give-aways that a relationship is faltering – if you can give yourself the distance to see them.

See IDEA 14, *Putting the past where it belongs*, on learning how to put the past behind you and get ready to meet someone new.

Try another idea...

- Communication dries up. The phone rings less frequently, and when he does call he is saying goodbye almost as soon as he has said hello. When you're together, you find yourself racking your brains for something to say and he doesn't do much in the way of making conversation. His sentences are short and he never elaborates when telling you about his day, nor does he make any jokes or share observations with you. Practically anything on TV is more interesting than you, even gardening shows.

- You can't do anything right. He now thinks that what was once his favourite top makes you look fat, your friends irritate him and he never laughs at your funny stories. Problems he once used to sympathise with, he now claims are all your fault. You drop a

'They always say that time changes things, but you actually have to change them yourself.'
ANDY WARHOL

Defining idea...

cup and it becomes an all-out screaming match. This is the 'bad cop' technique, where he is trying to provoke you into calling it off. If things are going this way, act fast. If you don't, not only will you end up feeling guilty for ending it, but you will also probably put up with it for long enough for you to start to feel bad about yourself. It's the meanest, weakest and most damaging way for someone to call things off, so watch out for it.

- He wants his life back. You are no longer issued an open invitation to everything he does, he doesn't tell you who just called him and he refers to himself, when making plans, as 'I' rather than talking about 'we'. He may as well pack a suitcase for you; this is a blatant message he is giving out.

How did it go?

Q My boyfriend does all the things you listed but denies wanting to split up. I am so confused. What's going on?

A *He could just be scared of change so doesn't want to actually say it. Try asking another question.*

Q Like what?

A *Like do you want him. Maybe you should take some time out to think about what you would like rather than what he's prepared to give you. Write a list of how it is versus how it should be.*

Q I think I love him. What if he leaves?

A *I love cake but it doesn't do me any favours. You get what you're prepared to settle for, so don't sell yourself short.*

25

What men want

OK, OK, let's keep it clean, ladies. Of course, all men want that, but there are some other qualities that men are looking for too.

And there are some universal truths about what men are after, just as there are for us women.

LOVE

Believe it or not, men are just as keen to make a connection as women are, they are just not as likely to confuse it with good sex. Someone to share things with, rely on and love comes high on many male lists. But don't confuse the desire to love with the desire to commit: that comes later.

DESIRE

They want you to want them as much as they want you: and, yes, they'll want you to think about embarking on any kind of relationship. You don't have to fit the standard-issue magazine model, but they do want someone who takes pride in how she looks and feels good about her own body. There's no bigger turn-off

Here's an idea for you... **As well as knowing a little more about the male mind, it might be a useful exercise to work out what qualities you would ideally like – and then try and make them a reality in your next relationship rather than hoping he's a mind reader.**

than someone waving their cellulite in your face and telling you how hideous it is – it's called negative marketing. Stop it. You can loll about the house in no make-up and your jogging bottoms and still appear attractive if you feel good doing it, but throw in greasy hair and some whining and you are on your own.

HAPPINESS

Happy people are like luck magnets; everyone wants to be around them, learn their secret, get happy osmosis. And while no one can be happy all the time, your world view is pretty important. Only the creepiest of men want a depressed woman around, usually so they can feel superior. If you do have personal issues then take control of them yourself; while it's totally appropriate to share your woes with your loved one, he's not your therapist. He needs some lifting up too.

FRIENDSHIP

This mustn't be confused with being like one of his mates. While men want the good stuff – loyalty, concern, fun, companionship – they don't necessarily want you outdoing them in a belching competition. And don't fake an interest in football if you haven't got any; they can always find someone else to go to the match with.

SUPPORT

Want to use your new insights? See IDEA 47, *Making anyone want you*, on how to find a man.

Try another idea...

Constant criticism is wearing, and an easy trap to fall into. Buoying up someone's spirits, being friendly to their friends or work associates, these are all ways of making someone feel treasured and supported. If you can do it without them having to remind you, this will also create more trust, a vital part of feeling valued.

SANITY

What once seemed exciting and off the wall soon becomes a hideous chore. A neurotic, clingy or shouting woman might be a sexy stereotype in a film but is a nightmare to have in your life as a friend or a partner. After all, the same qualities in a man would put you off, whereas a rational person, someone you can talk to and lean on at times, generates respect and trust. Being irrational shouldn't be confused with being a challenge. Mount Everest is a challenge, but no one wants to live on it.

CHALLENGE

So what is a good challenge? A woman who stands her ground and knows her own mind, being sharp enough to know when someone is trying it on and not becoming so acquiescent that she becomes almost invisible. If someone lets you down be clear about your feelings; men respond to direct statements (hysterics switch them off), and it shows that you think you're worth more. So they will, too.

'The male is a domestic animal which, if treated with firmness, can be trained to do most things.'
JILLY COOPER, British novelist

Defining idea...

103

CONSIDERATION

Shockingly, men respond to the same stuff as women! Who would have thought it? Tea in bed, making sure he has something in the fridge to eat when he gets home if he has to work late and offering to pick up medicine when he is ill... It may all seem like some weird, 50s-throwback behaviour, but these are the little acts of thoughtfulness that make a woman go weak at the knees when shown to her. The rest of the world is indifferent to his minor personal crises, so you shouldn't be. Of course, these acts should be returned, but studies show that acts of kindness make both the doer and the receiver feel good, so if you get the balance right you can both be nurtured and nurture. I can feel world peace just around the corner.

SPACE

Finally, men want space (and emotionally healthy women should too). Men want the room to make their own decisions, have their own private thoughts and sometimes just not think at all. Part of women's lifeblood is to always try and work out where things are at; men don't want that constant pressure. If you call him constantly at work, expect him to remember the name and love lives of your thirteen cousins *and* their cats, then you are actually expecting him to be a woman. That is what your best friend is for. Only teenage girls expect to share every intimate detail of their lives with their partners.

Q **I tried not calling my boyfriend at work and now I'm scared. He called me. What do I do?**

How did it go?

A *Er, isn't that good?*

Q **Yes, but I feel like I'm performing some weird voodoo magic. Why did it work?**

A *Because you gave him a chance to miss you. Nature hates a vacuum; give him space to make his own choices and if he loves you, he'll choose you. Then you can both be secure in that knowledge rather than both of you thinking he only calls back to avoid the grief.*

26

When to do the deed

Sex is a wonderful, essential part of many people's lives, and inextricably linked to dating.

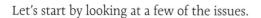

And the biggest question is when to go from dating to mating, and the right time has always been a topic of hot debate.

Let's start by looking at a few of the issues.

WHAT ARE YOU AFTER?

For some people, dating is about playing the field and trying out a few teammates. For others, it's a means to an end, a way to find a more steady, committed relationship. But there is also nothing to say that the two are mutually exclusive, though often they are. Work out what you want from dating: if it's just a couple of years being footloose and fancy free, then some no-strings sex and attention from some lucky men might be exactly what you need. However, if you are looking for something more permanent, you need to think more seriously about the sex choices you are making.

THE BIOLOGY

When women have sex, they release a hormone called oxytocin (also referred to as 'the cuddle hormone'), which, amongst other things, encourages a woman to feel

Here's an idea for you...

Take control of the messages you are sending out. If you want more than a one-night stand, don't take the conversation to sexy places you are not ready to go to. Flirt your heart out but don't recount the biology pages from the encyclopedia; it's not only confusing, it will make you look like a good-time gal rather than a good-relationship gal. Ask lots of questions about the other person's background and interests to let them know you want more than just physical fun.

connected to her partner, and feel a sense of well-being. This is really worth thinking about as it can mean that you feel 'attached' to someone you don't really know just because you have slept with them. It can cloud your judgement and stop you working out if they are really compatible. On an emotional level, some women can confuse the intimacy created during sex with something more meaningful; this is especially easy if you have been on your own for a while. If any of these ideas sound a note of truth with you, consider waiting a little while before you dive in. If you get on with your man, it will be better for the wait; if you go off him, it will make it easier to walk away.

GOOD GIRL VERSUS BAD GIRL SYNDROME

It shouldn't make a difference, in our enlightened age, what we choose to do with our bodies. But actions are interpreted differently by others, no matter what our intentions are. After quizzing many men, I have been categorically told that if you want a relationship you should hold off on having sex. How long is up to you, but sex on the first date is a definite no-no. This is directly related to the fact that men want to feel that the woman they are with was worth the chase. Holding back is more likely to make him think of you as girlfriend material than if you get out your whip before you know his second name. And letting a relationship have a slow sexual build also builds the intrigue and sexual excitement.

Of course, some people throw themselves into bed with great aplomb and are still together sixty years later, but that is more because they turned out to be well suited emotionally, than because they are living proof that you don't always ruin things by rushing them. Although I still believe that waiting is key, I also believe that when it *is* right, you can't get it wrong.

Take a look at IDEA 43, *Contraception choices*, for ideas on what to do should you decide to get physical.

Try another idea...

GREAT SEX TRAP

For some women, a good relationship counts for nothing unless the sex is great too, so a 'test ride' is an essential part of working out if they want to take things further. That's fine if you are both part-time international porn stars who are used to switching on an earth-shattering performance at the drop of a G-string. But lots of us take a little time to warm up and understand the body of someone new, so don't rule out the possibility of a replay just because you didn't see stars. Most couples report that sex improves as their knowledge of each other also does.

Of course, the flip side of this is that you may be the kind of person who loves the excitement and naughtiness that a one-night stand can give you. But you do have to think about whether this is serving you well if none of your liaisons ever turn into a relationship because you can only let go with a stranger.

'If sex is such a natural phenomenon, how come there are so many books on how to?'
BETTE MIDLER, US actress

Defining idea...

How did it go?

Q **I love sex, so why should I wait if we are both drawn to each other?**

A *Because getting sex is easy, but getting a lasting relationship needs a different approach.*

Q **But if he only judges me on being open-minded about sex then he's not for me. Right?**

A *Not everyone who has sex straight away is open-minded about it, in the same way that not every monogamous long-term sexual relationship is boring. Jumping into bed can suggest that this is your main priority, not a relationship.*

Q **Surely I can explain that I am interested in a relationship as well?**

A *Of course, and while you are at it bring along a bunny to boil, because you are going to sound desperate. No one wants to feel they are being shoved into the role of partner just because you want someone to be with. It's important to feel that someone wants you, not just someone to split the rent.*

Q **Help! So do I have to go without sex?**

A *No, have casual flings with whoever you want but if you meet someone special, treat him in a special way. You'll get back what you give out.*

27

Bad-news boys

Much as we would all like to believe that we're unique and that the mould was broken when they made us, blah blah blah, the reality is different.

People can be categorised as certain 'types'. Fine, if you're talking about the 'loving' or 'great at everything' type. But it's the other ones you've got to watch out for...

So as soon as the smart woman finds her date revealing himself to be one of the following, she's got to be climbing out the restaurant's toilet window. If it takes a little time for him to reveal his true nature, run twice as fast: he may be a Two Face – someone who knows how to be nice but only does it till he gets what he wants. The most deadly of the bunch. So Spot the Dog:

MARRIED MAN

Yes, it may see obvious but many a woman has fallen for the charms of someone else's man. After all, he's into commitment, right? Although some people do find the love of their lives whilst they are still with someone else, a good rule of thumb is that if someone doesn't leave their marriage within six months, they probably

Here's an idea for you... **If you feel unsure about a guy write down a pros and cons list then go one further – write down how it makes you feel. If you find, for example, 'lacking in confidence' coming up more than once you might be able to see that he has a system, even if he can't. Explain how it affects you and see if he is willing to work on it (it may be that no one has challenged it before) but if not, it's probably time to call it off.**

never will. In the meantime, you will still be the single girl at weddings, feeling cynical. Also, you've got to question this man's morals: if he treats her like this, he can – and probably will – do it to you. The only married man worth even considering is the one who tells you to leave him alone and he'll find you if/when he leaves his marriage.

DOMINATOR

After being on your own for a while, the Dominator can seem like a breath of fresh air. He takes an interest in all that you do, from the way you organise your cupboards to how your friends treat you; it's wonderful to have someone to share with. But pretty soon he is telling you that you fold the laundry wrong (although he never does any) and that your best friend is boring (he doesn't like anyone else to have any influence). Being a control freak is not about love, although he'll tell you it is: it's about power. And don't always expect him to come at you shouting: he might make his disapproval clear by whingeing at you ('Oh, not like that, you've spoilt it now'), or just indulging in low-level nitpicking. Leave, before your confidence does.

BROKEN HEART

The ex-girlfriend/mother/cat took him to the emotional cleaners and you are going to hear *all* about it. You will alternatively have to be blamed for/explain the actions of all womankind. Be prepared for a glazed look to come into his eyes every time you pass their favourite restaurant/old apartment/tree. There are two types of Broken Heart: the ones who are repairing it and who'll eventually recover, and the ones who live in a haze of self-indulgent gloom and who love the drama of their own misery. Basically, you are transitional woman in a nurse's uniform; if you like this guy, give him a wide berth and let him find another nurse. You have a much better chance of making it work if you are the girl *after* the girl *after* the girl before (get it?).

Look at **IDEA 28, *The phone stops ringing...,* for other men that need to be given the heave-ho.**

Try another idea...

SMOOTHIE

James Bond has nothing on this guy. He is as slick as an oil spill, and with just as many birds trapped in it. Restaurant? Booked. Flowers? Delivered, and in your favourite colour. Suits? Exquisite. Home? A spread from an interiors magazine. He may even tell you how much he loves and admires women. Note: womEN. Not womAN. And a man who thinks that people who are interchangeable because they have XX chromosomes is much more likely to be a misogynist; he can't see past the skirt to one special individual. In the old days, this guy was known as a good, old-fashioned bachelor. And he will remain so till he dies of a heart attack under some lissom nineteen-year-old.

THE DRAIN

Everything he does is a chore. Work's a nightmare, his friends are always trying to rip him off, he hates his life. This is a very common kind of Drain, one that relies on you to bolster

'When the character of a man is not clear to you, look at his friends.'
Japanese proverb

Defining idea...

113

his poor self-image constantly. But he's probably the least worrying; other Drains include men who always seem to be borrowing money because they have maxed out their credit cards, who lose their temper over nothing and use you as an emotional punchbag and those who use you as a real punchbag… You recognise a Drain because you feel drained when they finally leave the house. I hope I don't even have to tell you what to do here.

How did it go?

Q   I've met a great guy but he likes to tell me what to do. Are you saying I should just throw it away?

A   *Some people develop bad habits in the way they speak, and come home from work making everything into an order. If you think he is just one of these, explain to him that it makes you feel crowded and ask him to refrain. If he isn't a real dominator, he'll back off.*

Q   I don't want him to stop caring. Won't this do that?

A   *There is a middle ground; if he withdraws all attention and concern from you because you won't bend to his will, he is a Dominator. And they only get worse. There's a difference between Mr Right and Mr Right About Everything.*

28

The phone stops ringing...

Then it starts. Then it stops. And without the power of being able to see into the future, we are sometimes just playing 'wait and see'.

People get together for all kinds of reasons: company, attention, fun and sex being just some of them...

Sometimes it pans out, sometimes not: no real need for stress. Unless, of course, you are genuinely being used. Sad but true – there is a whole swathe of the male population just waiting to suck you dry... and not in a good way.

So how do you know if someone is sponging off you? Well, you will usually find out that one of your 'resources' suffers – your energy, finances, relationships with others, self-confidence – basically, the stuff that you use to renew and sustain yourself has suddenly been diverted off into his reserves. Check out this list of life-force suckers to see if any one of them rings any bells. Alarm bells.

THE LEANER

Oh, wouldn't you know it, his lease ran out, his car has died, his washing machine is broken. Can he stay, can he borrow your car, can he do a quick load in your

Here's an idea for you... **Not sure if your man fits into one of these categories or is guilty of something similar? Think you might be being a mug but can't decide? Switch places and imagine yourself asking him for the same favours or offering the same excuses. If you wouldn't demand it, don't give it.**

machine (using your washing detergent)? He would love to take you out to dinner but he can't afford to, as things are a bit tricky at work right now and he is worried he won't be able to meet his minimum payments on his staggering credit card debts... Before you know it, you are fretting about his finances and offering to work extra shifts (he can't because of his asthma). The most obvious drain here is of the hard cash sort, but the more insidious result of hooking up with a Leaner is that he will *never* get on the straight and narrow. If you kick him out, he'll take his boyish helplessness and find himself a new nurse before the door clicks closed, leaving you feeling like a mug. What seems like nurturing soon becomes carrying – so get rid of him immediately and if you still feel like taking care of something get a dog or a baby. Or a baby dog.

VERBAL DRIBBLER

Oh, being a teenager: remember how dramatic and exciting that all used to be? Sitting up into the small hours talking things out and putting the world to rights over a bottle of cheap red wine? But, of course, when you only had double maths or a general studies lecture to sit through it wasn't such a problem. As an adult, though, a guy who seems deep and sharing can quickly become a complete pain when you have to get up to a busy day at the office. If you find yourself being a vessel into which a man chooses to pour his woes endlessly, give him the number of a local therapist and move on. This man is a malcontent, and if he can't take responsibility for his own happiness, he won't take responsibility for playing a part in yours. If you find it hard to say goodbye, don't worry; just walk out mid-sentence. It will be a couple of hours before he realises you've left the room.

Take a look at **IDEA 27, Bad-news boys, on more men to avoid like the proverbial plague.**

Try another idea...

THE CLIMBER

What do you mean you want a birthday present? Wrapped? Can't you see how busy he is at work? How stressed he is, how important he is? If you weren't so self-absorbed you would see that he had to spend four nights a week entertaining clients/friends/contacts if he was going to close the deal/improve his chances/become president of the United States. A relationship with a man like this usually ends with him 'upgrading' to a partner who suitably reflects his status when that promotion finally comes. He gives you just enough to keep you at his side whilst he concentrates on world domination. Give him the widest berth possible.

HOT TEXTER

You have a date. It's great, you feel sexy, smart, funny and valued. You may or may not sleep together; either way, you expect to be hearing from him soon. Anytime now. Is the phone plugged in? You are sure he had a great time too, in fact, he said so... Just as you go off the boil, he texts you: something along the lines of how busy he has been/out of town due to a work emergency/caring for his sick hamster. You feel relieved and the flirty texts start up again; he can't meet up right now but would love to see you soon. Again, silence: only the sound of

'**There is nothing like a dream to create the future. Utopia today, flesh and blood tomorrow.**'
VICTOR HUGO, *Les Miserables*

Defining idea...

tumbleweed rattling through your bedroom to keep you company. Then a text, full of good wishes and chirpiness. You catching the theme here? This man is *not* interested in you; he is using these little vignettes of contact to puff up his weak ego just so he knows he can still get your attention should he want it. He feels good, you feel confused and unsettled; he is draining you. Block his number from your phone and refuse to play his game; you can't lose if you don't play.

Q   Uh oh. I think I may be going out with a Hot Texter. But he's the only love interest in my life right now. What's going on?

A   He's the love interest in his life. You are basically the spiritual equivalent of a hand job whilst he is waiting for someone he can actually be bothered to meet up on a proper date with.

Q   Why contact me at all, then?

A   Drunk, Friday night, bored, lonely, nothing on TV... Got the picture? Off you go, girl, you can do better.

Age concern

Suddenly a cutie catches your eye and you find yourself considering someone who never blipped on your radar before. Because they're not even nearly in your age group.

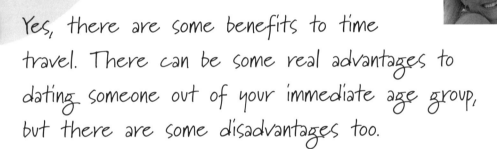

Yes, there are some benefits to time travel. There can be some real advantages to dating someone out of your immediate age group, but there are some disadvantages too.

CHILD'S PLAY

A younger man can have less baggage and fear holding him back from taking risks or trying new things; and can bring some much needed levity into your life after a heartbreak. Because younger men are not necessarily looking for a serious commitment or feeling any time pressure, you can enjoy the moment without measuring them up for a wedding suit.

Sounds great? Of course, but then, naturally, we've got to talk downsides. It might be that your date is lacking something in the life-experience department, the bedroom department (no, clitoris is not a Greek island), and the being-able-to-afford-expensive-dinners department. You may also find yourself making a dash for

The key to a fun time with a younger or older man is to acknowledge from the start that you *are* at different life, and experience, stages. Being pissed off because they still want to spend lots of time with their mates (younger) or don't want to take up white-water rafting (older) is your problem, not theirs. Be honest about what you want, if not with your partner, then at least with yourself. If you want a serious commitment or children, listen to what your liaison is telling you about his feelings rather than trying to persuade him. An older man knows his mind well enough not to want to compromise (especially if he has done it all before) and a younger man may resent the pressure if you try and make him do something for which he's not ready. Worst of all, you could have fallen hard for someone and then have to accept that you made a rod for your own back.

the loo in the middle of the night and confronting his flatmates – and an absence of toilet paper. And, of course, you may run the risk of hearing your body clock loudly tick tock babies when he isn't even ready to learn how to set an alarm clock for a steady job. Speaking of bodies: if you are insecure, younger men aren't always the best option. They may have watched too much MTV and not seen enough reality TV to understand the concept of gravity (or maybe they just haven't covered that in class yet).

VINTAGE MODEL

As for older guys, you will have the pleasure of being the pretty young thing. Those extra couple of pounds you obsess about will seem pretty desirable to an older bloke. He is more likely to have money to spend and his life in order, and know enough about relationships to be able to bypass a lot of the silly little niggles and insecurities that can plague a younger man. He also will have had all those dull conversations about foreplay – what it is, why they need to do it – which should make for an eventful bedtime (he won't have the 'frequency' of his younger brother but should have more going for him on the longevity front).

Take a look at IDEA 41, **Be the popular girl**, for ideas on finding yourself in the right place to meet guys of all ages.

Try another idea...

Of course, you could be a symptom of his mid-life crisis. Mid-life-crisis men are unlikely to want to hitch up with you for any length of time, and may have come out of a difficult break-up or divorce. As a result he may be looking to play about and cut a dash around town – so if you want someone to snuggle up on the sofa with and dream paint colours for the nursery, he may not be an ideal match. Speaking of nurseries, remember that he may come with baggage... This will affect everything about your relationship from when he's free to when you get to stay. Not that this is a terrible thing if he's the right guy; just remember that he might already have someone close to his heart, and only Cruella De Ville would want to shove those little (or fully grown) people out of the way.

There is, of course, the possibility that he is the eternal bachelor, and hasn't had a significant other for any serious length of time. By all means, lounge on his leather sofa, sip his expertly blended martinis (with olives), but don't try and sneak a toothbrush into his cabinet. This man is not waiting to meet the right woman, although he may be interested in the right housekeeper: someone who knows how to get a crease right.

'Boys will be boys, and so will a lot of middle-aged men.'
KIN HUBBARD, cartoonist

Defining idea...

IN IT FOR THE LONG HAUL

So it started as a bit of fun and now it has blossomed into a serious contender. In the face of a relationship that encompasses a generational disparity – either way – people are going to have opinions. Somewhere along the line, people are going to be frightened that someone might be taken advantage of. And if kids are involved (yours or his), you will need to allow everyone the opportunity to have room for change and acceptance. If it's right, they'll come around.

How did it go?

Q I met an older guy who is everything I want in someone my own age, but can't find. I get the feeling he doesn't want anything serious. Could I be right?

A   Trust your feelings. Sure, he knows how to open a door and comment on your outfit, but if he doesn't want what you want, saying it in a polite way won't make it any less frustrating.

Q   So should I hang in there or call it off?

A   If you can handle a little fun and attention, enjoy yourself. But if you think you might want more, don't hang around to see if you can change his mind. Unlike younger men, he probably knows what he wants, and probably won't budge.

30

Meeting the family

**Your relationship is ready to move on to the next level...
which for many means meeting the family.**

*The only way to deal with the family
meet and greet is to come up with a
serious game plan...*

So, you're dating, he's seen you naked and survived, he's probably even aware by now that your Saturday night pants and your Wednesday pants have nothing in common stylistically apart from elastic. Now for the ultimate test. The family. I don't know if the Greeks had a word for this but they should have done. It would have gone something like 'arrrghhhhh' and translated into 'embarrassment meets agony meets general low-level feelings of shame'. Unless, of course, your parents are an absolute joy, in which case they are possibly even odder than most.

Formulate your plan and stick to it.

POWER POWWOWS

First up, what is really going on here? Is your mum the kind of malcontent who won't like any boyfriend, regardless? Or is your dad a monosyllabic but well-meaning wallflower who balks at any kind of dialogue with anyone other than close blood relatives? Basically, know your limits. Feeling devastated because you didn't

Here's an idea for you... **If your parents live a good distance away and you need to make a weekend visit, ensure you build some time into it for just the two of you as a couple. The constant smile can give a person face-ache and meeting new people can be draining, so give him some time off. He'll love you for it.**

get the Waltons' reaction that you were hoping for is crazy if you didn't come from the Waltons (which, I can tell you, you didn't: they're not real). This is not the time to try and resolve the old psychodramas that have been playing themselves out in your family for years. Don't cry when your mum hates his shoes if she always finds something to criticise: your mantra here is 'anticipate and ignore'. Concentrate, rather, on making light of it with your boyfriend; if you think he has serious potential, surely you want him to be able to contemplate Christmas with them without running screaming into the night? The approval you are looking for – it should be from him.

BALL'S IN HIS COURT

Speaking of which, don't ever try and make a man meet your family unless he wants to – it's a sure-fire way of turning him off. Most people connect meeting the family with something serious, even if in your household your mum has had a cup of tea with every one-night stand you've ever had. It's bound to go badly if he spends the whole time coiled like a spring ready to deny impending nuptials. If he's the right one, you'll get there.

NEUTRAL TERRITORY

Next up, decide where to meet. If your dad is likely to drag him round the garden and show him his extensive vegetable patch for hours, you could always choose a restaurant to have dinner so the 'intimacy' isn't forced too soon. The advantage of this approach is, of course, that he doesn't get to see your time-capsule bedroom or gawky teenage photos. It can also give a time frame to the date ('Only four hours, I promise!') and

Work out if he's worth bringing home. Check out IDEA 52, *Are we there yet?*

Try another idea...

something else to discuss ('What exactly is a "jus" anyway? Is it just posh juice?'). This works especially well if your parents are difficult to handle – start fights with each other, ask you when you are going to get your moustache waxed – because it means the end is in sight for you too. You don't have to dance to their tune if you are not on their land.

BRIEF THE TROOPS

Tell your mum not to mention the fact that you get involved too quickly with every man you meet, and ask your dad not to grill your partner on his politics if you think it might be a hot topic. Also throw them all a bone: 'Dad, Phil loves car racing,' or let your mum know his favourite dish if she's cooking – it breeds goodwill all round. (As does making sure he buys a bottle of wine or some flowers.)

You need to prepare him for the big stuff. Don't shy away from mentioning the fact that your mother likes a gin and tonic, or several, rather than have him discover it as she falls into the pot plants. Even if you don't want to bring it up, it will be a much harder conversation to have after you have let him discover it the hard way. But make sure that you are not so honest that he turns up wanting to kill them all for being totally cruel and evil to you when you were five. Once you have started the hatred wheel rolling, it's hard to stop it.

'Happiness is having a large, loving, caring, close-knit family in another city.'
GEORGE BURNS

Defining idea...

127

STOP CRINGING

Finally, there are limits to what you can do. Your parents may have brought/dragged you up but you are not interchangeable with them. If they act badly, goose the waiting staff or ask your man in-depth questions about his finances, try and let it go. After all, he isn't going to be spending all his time with them, now, is he? Grown-up men know that all is not perfect and would support, rather than berate, you for having bonkers parents.

How did it go?

Q   **We are going home to meet my folks next week and I am really nervous. Can you help?**

A   *Talk it through with your man. He may be able to reassure you and let you know he will still like you, whatever.*

Q   **But we are a really close family and he might not fit in. How do I make sure he does?**

A   *Two things: one, cut the apron cord, your relationship can only cope with the responsibility of you two getting along before you need him to be in love with the whole family, and two, time out! You have more than twenty-four hours to get this right. Don't make this meeting so pressured; you can do it again and again and again...*

31
Money – the sticky stuff

Modern dating's a confusing world, not least because many women are independent, don't need escorts to be allowed out and can afford to buy their own handbags.

So, as well as the old-fashioned rules about who asks who out, we also have the thorny issue of who picks up the bill...

As a rule of thumb, whoever asks for the date should be the one to pay. However, money is not neutral and you need to think about what kind of message you are sending out when you make your decision.

HUNTER-GATHERING STUFF

Many men feel uncomfortable if a woman wants to pay; it's their last vestige of masculinity when it comes to feeling like a provider (don't laugh, it's an important part of a normal man's identity). You may think you are being fair, wanting to take turns at picking up the bill, but life's a bit more complicated than that. You also need to consider the balance that you are creating: you can't complain that he doesn't treat you like a princess if you take away every opportunity for him to do so.

Here's an idea for you...

Play the credit card shuffle. Sometimes on a date you may feel that it is entirely appropriate to pay half, or all, of the bill. Maybe you asked him out, or the date was so wrong for you that you want to leave without any pressure to see him again. One way of getting around the thorny issue of arguing over who pays for what is to catch the maître d' on your way to the toilet and give him your card directly. But if the bill comes to the table, you can simply leave it till the last minute and slip your card in the billfold as you hand it to the waiter, taking it out of your date's hands. If he argues with you, consider letting him pay; springing for dinner doesn't count for much these days, and if he seems to think it does, remind him that they have a word for that – prostitution.

Of course, some guys want to be the princess. Which is fine, as long as he buys his own crown – watch out for a man who never pays his way or treats you.

However, you may have fallen for a fledgeling photographer who has yet to make any money, while you are riding high on your expense account. The most important thing here is to show compassion; you can't expect flashy dinners all the time, even if you are willing to pay, without making him feel marginalised. So try a picnic in the park or trips to a gallery that he can stump up for, or he will get tired of being the poor relation and move on. There is no denying that money is power and must be handled with care to stop it causing rifts.

COUGHING UP

Talking about money is really difficult for most people: it is an emotional issue and cited as one of the key issues in relationship breakdowns. So the sooner you get comfortable with it, the sooner you can get over any awkwardness. That's not to say that you should ask to see his bank statements within the first week, but you should be capable of being frank as things develop. What happens if he moves into your flat? Will he want his name on the mortgage if he's paying

For other ways that you might be kidding yourself, take a look at IDEA 35, *Are you a psycho?*

Try another idea...

towards it? Maybe he's much wealthier than you: have you found yourself living beyond your means to keep up? You'll hit the ground hard when it's over... Getting these thorny issues upfront could save you both a lot of hurt later.

WHAT'S YOUR DEAL?

So what is your own feeling about money and men? Money is often a great way of working out where you are at in many ways. Firstly, if you are a spender with credit cards mounting up all over the shop, you may be looking for someone to bail you out: not exactly the most romantic way to find a soulmate. Alternatively, you may have your chequebook tightly balanced and be unwilling to hook up with a guy who has debt; prudence is always a good thing but with things like student loans and stag nights being held in expensive locations, you might easily meet someone with problems. My surprising money issue was that I'd made myself so independent and secure, and liked to take turns to pay for dinner, that I didn't realise I was using it to keep men at arm's length. I thought I was being responsible and capable but, what do you know, it was fear dressed up in a pretty hat. Money isn't a neutral issue so it is unlikely that your approach to it will be, either. Think about how it informs your emotional decisions.

'A wise man should have money in his head, but not in his heart.'
JONATHAN SWIFT

Defining idea...

133

How did it go?

Q **I really like a guy but he never has any money. Every date we go on he complains about how bogged down he is with student debt and car payments and other such worries.**

A *Run for the hills. This guy is the worst kind of debtor, the one who thinks none of it is his fault. People only get out of debt when they take responsibility for it. He's too immature to see cause and effect; if he can't meet his car payments he shouldn't have a car.*

Q **So you don't think it will change?**

A *Not unless he does, and that would take effort, so I doubt it. It might not seem so bad now, but it will when there are hungry children to feed.*

Q **Seems harsh to just give up; should I?**

A *Offer to work out a budget with him, as he might truly just be overwhelmed, and then see if he actually tries to stick to it. Whatever you do don't lend him money, or you'll join his debt spiral.*

32

Breaking up is hard to do

Sometimes it just isn't there. You have pushed, prodded and tried to shoehorn this person into a relationship, but it just isn't going to work.

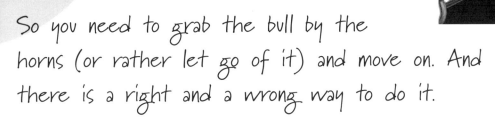

So you need to grab the bull by the horns (or rather let go of it) and move on. And there is a right and a wrong way to do it.

Getting it right lets both of you move on with dignity and calm, but getting it wrong can leave you both licking your wounds and making voodoo dolls for months, if not years, to come.

HOW TO SPLIT UP WITH A GOOD ONE

Oh, if only it was possible to flip the X factor like a light switch. Sometimes it just doesn't work and you've got to cut a nice guy loose. The best way to deal with men like this is face to face and showing them the respect they deserve, even if it makes things a little harder for you. That way they, and you, can rest assured that you did the dignified thing. But once you are sitting opposite, what do you say?

- Don't lie. Making up a dead aunt or work stress is unfair. If they have done right by you don't slope off under the cover of a fib; they will probably be able to tell and worry about what else you have lied to them about.

135

Here's an idea for you... **If you think a break-up may turn ugly, do it in a public place and have a friend come and meet you at a prearranged time. That way, you are making a clear statement that the meeting is over.**

- Be as honest as you can be. If the spark is just missing, tell them that. It's not uncommon for lots of things to be right but one thing to be wrong and you can even commiserate with them; chances are if you aren't feeling it, they won't be either.

- Don't suggest it might happen further down the line. If they really like you they will keep hanging in there waiting for you to change your mind, which is stopping them from finding someone else. No matter how reassuring for you it would be to have a nice guy waiting in the wings in case you don't find Mr Right, it's wrong, wrong, wrong...

- Answer any questions with the best framing possible. When people are upset they may level a lot of hurt questions at you; try not to respond in kind. If they ask if it was because you didn't like their knobbly chicken legs, don't start clucking. You can simply say you didn't feel a sexual chemistry; after all, one woman's chicken legs are another woman's lean, athletic pins. There is no point in dashing his confidence. At the same time, if his fifteen phone calls a day did irritate you, you could let him know. It might stop him from making the same mistake again.

- Balance criticism with positivity. If you are going to mention the fifteen calls a day, then make sure that you let him know that while being attentive was great, it could be moderated (not stopped). You don't want to release him onto an unsuspecting female population imagining that the best way to take things forward is never to pick up the phone.

- Don't use them for ex sex. What for you is just a convenient lay, might keep their hurt alive and erode their confidence, whilst fostering false hope.

IDEA 36, *Valium and valentines*, can remind you why no relationship is better than a dead one.

Try another idea...

- Don't tell them how they feel. You have had time to get used to the idea; it's news to them and they may feel disappointed or that you had more potential.

- Stick to your guns. Just because they think you still have something between you if you really haven't, keep reminding them that you don't think that it's the case. You will only have to go through this again further down the line. And do you really want people lying in bed at night trying to interpret what you said? Heartless!

- Try not to get defensive. If they start blaming you, keep calm and don't blame them back. They will start brooding on what you have said when the dust has settled and may find it hard to let it go.

HOW TO SPLIT UP WITH A BAD ONE

Well, I'm showing my dark side here, but who cares? If someone has been mean or destructive towards you, they are not entitled to any respect in return. The problem is that sometimes our judgement gets a little bit clouded. I suggest that if you aren't sure, just keep it short and sweet. If they are real meanies, and have left you hanging on for

'Saying goodbye doesn't mean anything. It's the time we spent together that matters, not how we left it.'
TREY PARKER and MATT STONE, creators of *South Park*, the US cartoon show

Defining idea...

137

phone calls/stood you up/left you dying of thirst in a desert, try some of the silent treatment back. A few days in dating no-man's-land waiting for the phone to ring might teach these men a few lessons about empathy. And if they hate you for it, who cares? Save your good stuff for those who deserve it.

How did it go?

Q I told this lovely guy I met it wasn't going anywhere and he still keeps sending flowers and calling. What can I do?

A *Were you totally clear?*

Q Well, I said the timing was off. I was pressured at work. Is that what you mean?

A *Duh! This may make him think he needs to redouble his efforts. Do the honourable thing and be unequivocal and exact with him; it's like ripping off a plaster, it will hurt you both more initially but you'll both recover faster. I know you thought he would get the hint but if it was a guy doing it to you we'd be slagging him off for cruelty. Be a woman about this and find your backbone; you will both feel more dignified for it.*

33

Getting over rejection

Along with the highs and the fun of dating, comes some of the rough stuff.

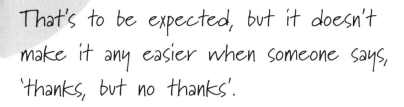
That's to be expected, but it doesn't make it any easier when someone says, 'thanks, but no thanks'.

The key to enjoying dating is to accept that just as everyone you meet can't light your fire, you're not everyone's idea of petrol either. But that's all very well in theory. You need some practical tools to make sure that you can stay afloat when buffeted by romance's vagaries.

SMILE, SMILE, SMILE!

When someone wants to make a break, let them go. Even if you think someone is making a mistake and there is potential in your relationship, no one normally wants to be anyone else's jailer. By all means, ask some questions if you think it will help, but don't plead, beg or whine. You'll be glad you kept your dignity when the initial discomfort has paled. Help is at hand…

- *Where is it coming from?* You've only had three dates and you feel like you will never get over the rejection? This guy probably isn't the reason; hell, you don't

Here's an idea for you...

If you are finding it hard to get over the knock to your confidence, try going somewhere where taking risks is all part of some good harmless fun. Speed-dating is a good way to see that this is all just a numbers game, to some degree; your right number just hasn't come up yet.

even know this guy. You may just have some old feelings that are coming up to do with your own confidence; a man shouldn't have this much effect so early on; you may need to look more closely at your own demons. You may also worry that he was your last shot at children, a home, someone to strut down the aisle with. This is just fear talking. Relax, you *will* get another shot at fulfilling your dreams.

- *Letting go of control.* You might think that if you had tried a different technique, worn different clothes or could just have one more chat with him you could turn things around. You can't. The great thing about being in a relationship is that two willing people choose it; once you can accept that you can't control everything, you can enjoy the fact that you aren't responsible for everything either.

- *Get back in the swing.* If someone wanted to end a brief fling, catching a glimpse of you sloping round the supermarket in your pyjamas will just reaffirm their conviction. It also means that the fantastically handsome guy fumbling through the meals for one is only going to speak to you to ask you where the air fresheners are. Even if you don't feel perky, act it: before you know it, the balance will be less act and more reality.

- *What were you expecting?* Something to do every Saturday night? Someone to rely on? Maybe you need to get a life that doesn't revolve around someone else and theirs. You will be much more likely to take rejection and break-ups more easily if your whole social structure isn't hinged around the other person.

■ *Don't put words in his mouth.* Don't imagine that you know what he is thinking. You don't know whether he wants to get back with his ex or try naked wrestling with his best friend Stuart. The point is, he doesn't want you and the worst kind of guy you can try and get involved with is one that doesn't really want you. You could get arrested for it, but worse, you could spend pointless months, years even, staring at the ceiling in the small hours of the morning trying to work out what went wrong when he doesn't even remember your name.

Have a look at IDEA 37, *Busting the bad days*, on how to cope with the gloomy blues.

Try another idea...

■ *Get the chocolate out.* Get the duvet on the sofa, have a good sob, drink a glass of wine and eat some chocolate all the while berating this fool that can't see what a prize you are to your most supportive mate. A knock to the confidence deserves a little ego stroke. Then get up tomorrow and move on.

And finally, remind yourself what this is about. Dating in itself is not a solution to all your problems, but then neither should a man be. Remind yourself that you are meant to be having fun and taking a few risks. Then put on your best outfit and hit the dance floor again.

Defining idea...

'*Finish each day and be done with it. You have done what you could. Some blunders and absurdities no doubt crept in; forget them as soon as you can. Tomorrow is a new day; begin it well and serenely and with too high a spirit to be cumbered with your old nonsense.*'
RALPH WALDO EMERSON, US essayist and poet

How did it go?

Q   OK, I hear what you are saying, but I had a great date with this guy and he gave me the total brush off. I feel totally humiliated. Now what?

A   *Do you have the power of second sight?*

Q   Erm, not last time I checked. What d'you mean?

A   *So why are you assuming it's something to do with you?*

Q   Because if it wasn't he would have called me again, wouldn't he?

A   *Or he may have realised from being on a date that he's not over his ex or that you're too fabulous for just a fling, and he isn't ready to commit.*

Q   OK, I prefer that theory. Is it right?

A   *Well, it is a theory but just as likely to be true as any of the others you may come up with, so why not choose to believe a dream instead of a nightmare? And then get on with something else; that man is gone.*

34

Here comes the sun

What a wonderful invention. The holiday romance...

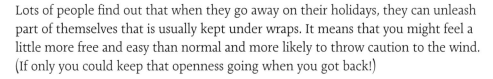

You don't have to bother with work, every night is a weekend night, and there's no one looking over your shoulder making sure you go home alone and eat sensibly.

Lots of people find out that when they go away on their holidays, they can unleash part of themselves that is usually kept under wraps. It means that you might feel a little more free and easy than normal and more likely to throw caution to the wind. (If only you could keep that openness going when you got back!)

A LITTLE LOVIN' IN THE SAND

Sun-kissed flesh, tousled hair, outfits you could fit in your fist... oh, it's a veritable crime not to give in to the temptations of the flesh when the sun is shining. It can also make for a great sensual connection as you feel less inhibited by real life. But if you are a terminal romantic, this can combine with your nature to turn something that should be no more than a fling into a lasting relationship. If you play it smart, though, you could either get a great little confidence booster, or come back with

Here's an idea for you... **Think you might want more but not sure? Ask for his contact address but don't give yours; then wait two weeks to see if your interest fades like your tan. If it's up to you to initiate contact, you don't get entangled if you aren't interested, and will have him crazy with longing if you are.**

something (or someone) that could well outlast your summer tan. Apparently more people in their thirties meet partners on holiday than those in their twenties; ideal if you've exhausted your local bars.

THE RIGHT KIND OF SOUVENIR

This checklist should help you keep perspective:

- When you meet someone on holiday, remember that their constant availability, willingness to buy the drinks and happy-go-lucky demeanour is not necessarily their usual personality; you are in holiday warp. Holiday warp is where time gets crushed into an intense little bubble that bears no resemblance to real life. Things feel more urgent and special because the clock is ticking. So watch out for the warp effect before asking him and his entire family to move into your house back home.

- Your holiday type may not be your home-life type. Do you really have something in common apart from a love of duty free? Do you have similar goals and aspirations? Not an issue if you are having a week-long wrestle, but think on this before planning a rematch on home soil.

- Always use a condom. The last thing you want to remember him by is an unpleasant itch and an hour spent in stirrups.

- Ah, the locals, they are so friendly. Fallen for a local boy? Be realistic before you let your heart go; you could be one of many lovely girls to trip through his bedroom door during the summer. If it does seem to have potential, then factor the cost of flights and long-distance phone calls into your equation. Not to mention the trials of long-distance relationships: the nights alone when you need a hug, missing friends' birthdays because you are dashing away every weekend, the cultural differences you may have to overcome ('What do you mean, the men in your family don't clean?'). But if you still think it's worth a shot, good luck to you; you could be starting a whole new adventure.

Take a look at IDEA 47, *Making anyone want you*, for how to catch a lucky guy's eye with just the right flirty moves; on holiday you haven't got time to waste.

Try another idea...

- Don't reveal too much. Even if you want to show him your tan lines, you don't have to write your home address and email account down within the first few hours. Keep things light if you really are just looking for a fling, or you could find yourself on the move again when you get back – in hiding from your new stalker.

- Don't ditch your mates. It's so easy to get carried away on holiday, especially if you have been in need of the company of a loving man for some time. But don't forget it if you came away with a friend – and while it's fine to date, if she had wanted to be on her own on holiday she could have gone on a retreat. If you aren't careful, you could end up coming home to one less friendly supporter than you had when you left.

'He who would travel happily must travel light.'
ANTOINE DE SAINT-EXUPERY,
French writer, poet and aviator

Defining idea...

145

AFTER CHECK IN, REALITY CHECK

So you came home, and before you know it, you are running up your credit card seeing him and mooching with each other lovingly. Bear in mind, however, that you haven't seen each other in a stressful situation, getting ready for a meeting, late for work, too tired to make conversation and trying to find a 'clean-enough' pair of tights. (You, not him. Although that may be another surprise you have yet to discover.)

How did it go?

Q   I really liked a guy I met on holiday and I am pretty sure it was mutual, but a week later, still no call... What do I do?

A   OK, apply the one-call rule: everyone deserves the benefit of the doubt, and he may genuinely have lost your number, so make a single, chatty, friendly call and leave it up to him after that.

Q   OK, left a message. Still no return call. Well?

A   Then chalk it up to a happy holiday fling and try not to read too much into it. He may have a family back home which would make yours a lucky escape, or just not want to try anything serious. Get out and use that tan on someone new.

35

Are you a psycho?

Oh, yes. It's very easy to point the finger at the crazies and laugh, imagining that you are perfect in every way.

There is, of course, another way of looking at things. It's called reality.

It's very hard for us to see our own weaknesses or flaws, and very easy to demand that we should be accepted the way we are. But if you look closely, you may see a common theme in your relationships. Do you always decide you're bored just as the other person wants to move in? Do you find yourself leaving phone messages that never get answered? Does every guy just want to end up being 'friends?' You need to ask yourself why and consider making a change. I mean, I know they are men but it can't *all* be their fault.

Here are a few examples of the way we push love away in ways we least expect.

THE SHOE SLUT

You have a pair of shoes for every occasion, and then some. You get twitchy at the hint of a footwear sale and spend holidays looking for the perfect flat beach sandal. When they come through the door, your credit card bills now make the same sound as a telephone directory as they hit the mat. You are always on the phone

Here's an idea for you... **Take a clean sheet of paper and write down all your relationships and all of their good and bad points. The bad ones might give you an idea of what you need to work on (communication, for example); and the good (such as great cuddling or laughing together) will remind you that you can enjoy yourself, and to try and get the opposite of all that bad stuff onto your list.**

moaning to a friend about your inability to make your credit card payment/pay the rent/get that latest pair of Jimmy Choos. Honey, you are in a financial mess and only the Sultan of Brunei is going to be able to save you, and even he may have problems meeting your monthly outgoings.

Flip it. Get some help, now. No one wants to hook up with a liability. The chances are that you are scared, inexperienced or just totally have your head in the sand when it comes to money. Take control and make an appointment to see an independent financial advisor today. Swap your credit cards to interest-free ones and hawk the stuff you haven't been wearing on eBay. You are likely to have started shopping as a way to fill a void; but how can someone fill it if you've crammed it full of shoes?

THE WHINER

Life is awful. Your boss hates you, your dog ate your new handbag, you missed the bus, you can't get over your ex, your fish died when you were twelve... Need I go on? According to some, luck is dished out fairly randomly in life and the chances are, you get the usual mix of good and bad. But can you see it? Of course not. You are only ever looking for the stuff you can whine about because it's a short cut to getting some attention and not having to do anything about your life. You don't want a boyfriend, you want a crutch.

Flip it. Put an elastic band round your wrist and twang it every time you hear yourself start a conversation with a whining tone in your voice. If you think of something negative,

IDEA 44, *Live sexy*, will help you work out how to get nearer to living the life you want.

Try another idea...

challenge yourself to come up with an alternative good thing (I have fat thighs, for example, but my ankles look like they belong on a sparrow). You are reprogramming your brain to find the good, and soon that will be easier than finding the grotty. And easier on your wrists.

MS GOODBYE

It's just so strange. You've had some lovely relationships with wonderful men but none of them ever seem to pan out. How odd. Just as things are about to move on to the next level you find yourself un-attracted to them, arguing, so stressed at work you never have any time to see them. Will you ever meet Mr Right? The question should be whether you'll ever meet Mr Wrong... You are addicted to the first rush of love endorphins and you find ways to bring things to a close so you can start afresh. Yes, women can be commitment-phobes too.

Flip it. Admit you have a problem. Acknowledge that you behave so badly that they have to pull the plug, then write a plan of what you would like, and see the steps you need to work through (living together might be one). If you want to have a series of lovers rather than be tied down, that's great, but if

'Facts are stubborn things; and whatever may be our wishes, our inclinations, or the dictates of our passion, they cannot alter the state of facts and evidence.'
JOHN ADAMS, *Argument in Defense of the Soldiers in the Boston Massacre Trials*

Defining idea...

you want to get to the marriage and baby stage, you need to see the cause and effect of your actions. Running off just as things get serious won't do it – trust me, the grass isn't greener over there, it's just different grass.

How did it go?

Q   **I'm horrified. I didn't realise that I am total Ms Goodbye. I always thought it was them calling it off but now I see I pushed them to it. What does it mean?**

A   *Ah, the mind works in wonderful ways to help us get what we want – in your case, freedom.*

Q   **Good point, but I always thought I wanted to settle down. Was I wrong?**

A   *Wanted to or should? At the very least you can stop thinking you were always dumped and accept control, then think about what you really would like to happen next. You may surprise yourself with the answer.*

36

Valium and valentines

There are holidays, celebrations and festivals that all seem to have been designed to drive a single person insane.

Such as Valentine's Day — it should be renamed 'At My Lowest Ebb Day'. But these things come round every year, like clockwork, so you need a way to defuse the bombs.

It's time to take a look at the myth versus the reality. In our most vulnerable hours, it's a woman's way to imagine that all around are living the dream while we're enduring the nightmare. So if you are tempted to start visualising the fantasy and counting the paracetamol, try looking at these alternative versions.

VALENTINE'S DAY

Let's start with the biggie. The single person's Waterloo.

Myth: Couples wander under twinkly lights by the river watched by the smiling, round-faced moon, arms bowing under the weight of stylish flowers, on their way to a sweet bistro ('their' bistro...) for a candle-lit feast of figs and oysters, before retiring home to make sweet, sweet love.

Here's an idea for you... **If you have any low-level misery thoughts sifting through your brain, get a Woody Allen film out, realise that everyone has to navigate relationship dramas whatever their situation, then enjoy the peace and quiet in your very own home.**

Reality: It's a wet Tuesday night. He is driving from garage to garage in a panic looking for flowers/a card without the word 'willy' on it/a giant bar of chocolate, or anything that will pass for thoughtfulness. Face it, anyone passing most restaurants on this night could hear a fork drop, as lots of couples stare into their soup in silence and wish they could be at home watching paint dry. The only misty-eyed person is the restaurant owner, who hiked up his prices for his valentine special: a free glass of bad cava for every table booked.

CHRISTMAS

The time for family, say your ovaries, ticking loudly.

Myth: It's Christmas Eve. A woman in a tight lambswool sweater with perfect breasts and shiny hair laughs in a tinkly fashion as she unwraps emerald earrings which glint in the candlelight. She kisses her ski-tanned husband before they ascend the broad stairs to fill the stockings at the foot of their infants' beds. She returns downstairs to put the chicken inside a goose inside a turkey and all in the low heat of the Aga, for the assorted loving family arriving tomorrow. The gentle snow caresses the window panes. Even Aunt Sally gets a kiss under the mistletoe from Grandfather Joe as the men do the washing up while the women make room for a game of Monopoly with the children.

Reality: A woman in a stained silk blouse ('Where the hell is that bloody apron?!') hops around the kitchen as the smell of singed forearm fills the air. It's 3 a.m. but she doesn't want his critical mother to see her lack of organisational skills. He's asleep on the sofa after spending Christmas Eve in the pub with his five-a-side team. Happily, he will be awakened in half an hour by the kids, desperate to open the presents she's only just finished wrapping. In tin foil. She's drunk all the cooking sherry and is now eating liqueur chocolates by the fistful. The family arrives and immediately complains about the lack of parking/strange method of cooking carrots/unpolished cutlery. Everyone eats till they are sick, Aunt Sally gets felt up by Grandpa Joe but luckily everyone is drunk so she thinks she fell onto the Christmas tree. All the men pass out on the sofas leaving the women nowhere to sit; kids on a caffeine high from tons of chocolate and fizzy drinks are marauding around the house. Someone is quietly weeping over old family feuds. No one does the washing up.

For ways of picking yourself up when you just can't see the funny side take a look at IDEA 37, *Busting the bad days*.

Try another idea...

PUBLIC HOLIDAYS

Dark times in a singleton's life.

Myth: Gorgeous, lithe couples in expensive underwear whizz along in a car with the roof down, towards a towering country mansion where a four-poster bed, strewn with petals, awaits. They tumble in through the doorway and have barely opened the chilling champagne before desire has them hitting the sheets and the multiple orgasms.

'I finally figured out the only reason to be alive is to enjoy it.'
RITA MAE BROWN, US author and social activist

Reality: If they had planned a romantic weekend, then no one booked anything. If they did book something, then they spend their time worrying about pronouncing the name of the wine properly. They have to vacate their room by 10 a.m. They then spend several hours in rush-hour traffic sniping at each other. More likely, they have to make the obligatory trip to see their parents.

BIRTHDAYS

Wish you had someone to share it with? Get real.

Myth: Following a breakfast of champagne and smoked salmon, she arrives at work flushed. Flowers arrive every half hour, to envious glances from her workmates. She changes into the new dress he has bought for her, then is whisked to a meal he has cooked himself.

Reality: She has been slowly boiling with rage all day as there's been no card and no flowers are delivered to her desk at work. He hasn't booked anything and suggests he gives her his credit card number to get herself a present. After hysterics on the phone, he buys a blouse her mother would find frumpy and which is six sizes too large. She goes out with her friends and gets pissed instead.

Q   **Busted, I always imagine that everyone else is happy but me. Are they?**

How did it go?

A   *Of course not.*

Q   **But now I feel depressed that everyone is miserable. Is that the case, then?**

A   *Not true either. But what's the point in thinking negative thoughts when you already feel vulnerable? This is just to remind you that being in a relationship isn't the same as being happy. Anyone can be happy.*

37

Busting the bad days

No matter how much you want to keep on the sunny side of the street, being single (like being in a relationship) can have its down days.

But there are a few tricks to help you get out of the doldrums and moving again.

Sometimes your energy just gets low and you get a bit blue. That's fine, it's a regular part of life, but just in case you get sick of yourself being heartsick, here's what to do about it.

FULFIL A FANTASY

Or at least, make a start on it. If you loved riding horses as a kid and keep thinking that you would like to take it up again as a replacement for your Saturday morning hangovers, do some research and find out the nearest stables, and book a lesson. It will make you feel more in control and have the added advantages of getting you out of a rut you might have got into (like the Friday night drinking fest), of you losing some weight (from the sport and reduced alcohol intake) and of helping you meet some new people. There might even be a stable hand in it for you.

Here's an idea for you... Get an endorphin rush; a spot of exercise might be the last thing you think you want, but nature's own hormone rush will immediately lift your mood. If dragging your backside to the gym seems like too much hard work, do some hard-core cleaning such as finally getting to the back of the cupboards or those dusty skirting boards. Do it for at least an hour to feel the benefits – an improved mood as well as a clean house. Bonus.

BOOK A HOLIDAY

And not some bog-standard trip that you take every year. Is there a book you have read that is set in a wonderful location that captures your imagination? Do some internet surfing or plan an itinerary; if you want to go somewhere exotic try some practical research such as finding out the necessary jabs or visas to make you feel that you're a little closer to making the fantasy a reality.

TREAT YOURSELF LIKE A PRINCESS

Instead of waiting for a guy to come along and make you feel special, you can get a head start by doing it for yourself. (This also has the added advantage of, when that man does come along, making him think that this is the kind of behaviour you are used to and deserve.) Little touches can make you feel special: using an expensive fabric conditioner, eating fresh pineapple for breakfast, getting up five minutes earlier to make some real coffee. Make the everyday things in your life a little bit more film star and you'll feel like one.

STRETCH YOURSELF

Is there something that you have always thought of yourself as being bad at? Would you quite like to be able to spend a weekend in Paris and be able to order dinner in French? Face up to your demons and give it a go; you'll feel amazing once you've achieved it and busted the myth that you can't do whatever you put your mind to.

Take a look at **IDEA 41**, *Be the popular girl*, on perking up your social life.

Try another idea...

DO SOME GIRL MAINTENANCE

No matter how sloth-like you feel, once you start shaving, creaming and preening, you will become absorbed in the task and start to enjoy the results. Do more than your everyday routine; spend some real time holed up in the bathroom having an intensive hair pack or face steam. If that seems like too much effort then hand the responsibility over to somebody else: the professionals. Get yourself to the hairdresser and get a good blow dry (major hair decisions should never be taken in a negative frame of mind). Have a massage, your eyelashes dyed or a pedicure; you don't have to undergo expensive treatments to feel the benefit of investing in yourself and getting some undivided attention. Of course, a day at a spa would also be a wonderful way to make your little black cloud disperse.

LEAVE THE DISHES

On bad days you can stress and berate yourself for all the things that you should be doing, like the washing up, cleaning the kitchen floor and dropping off the dry cleaning. If you just don't feel like it, hell, no one died from an un-dry-cleaned skirt. So give yourself a day off and go for lunch with a friend.

'I am more and more convinced that our happiness or unhappiness depends far more on the way we meet the events of life, than on the nature of those events themselves.'
WILHELM VON HUMBOLDT, German diplomat and philologist

Defining idea...

159

CREATE A LIST OF REWARDS

It's also important to make sure that you see the results of your hard work, results that aren't related to what you are trying to achieve. If you have decided that you would like to lose weight, think about unrelated treats (rewarding yourself with cake will miss the point). Maybe it's a trip to a spa, a roller disco with your best friend or a day at the beach making yourself sick on rides.

HAVE A ROMANCE AMNESTY

Take a day off from fretting about a man. You can get back on your man strategy tomorrow.

How did it go?

Q   I'm sure I'd have fewer bad days if I could just get a man. Right?

A   *Well, unless he's Merlin the Magician, he's unlikely to eradicate them from your life completely.*

Q   But surely it would just be better if I met someone, wouldn't it?

A   *So in the meantime you are just going to wallow in misery? Very attractive, no wonder you have men beating down your door to share in it.*

Q   Funny. What, then?

A   *Learning how to improve your quality of life and change your mood for the better is a powerful skill; you might even be able to use it on Merlin when he has a tough day at the cauldron.*

38

Love across the photocopier

Work may be a four letter word, but the wonderful thing about it is that as well as bringing home your pay, you may end up bringing home a husband.

You have a very high chance of meeting your partner at work and as a result you need to make sure that you spend some time honing your pulling skills.

WHY DOES WORK WORK?

Remember when you were at school and boyfriends were two a penny? It seemed that the supply was endless and you only had to open the door to the library and you could fall over a new romance. Well, that was because you got the chance to know people; all right, those exchanges might have been as deep as finding out that they listened to soft rock in their bedrooms while weight training, but you also got to see them borrow pencils in maths or burn sausages in home economics class. The way that we live now, we are meant to discern everything about a possible partner in less than five minutes in a crowded bar and decide if they are a love match. Work takes you back to a place where not every exchange is loaded with pressure and an

It is worth finding out if your employer has a ban on workplace dalliances. Some places do, so bear that in mind. You could find yourself hauled up in front of Human Resources and hot under the collar for all the wrong reasons.

attraction can slowly build. And there's nothing more exciting when you finally confirm the fact that both of you seem to be making fifteen coffees a day at exactly the same time for exactly the same reason.

STRATEGIES FOR GETTING DOWN TO BUSINESS

The best way to think about an office romance is in business terms: as well as a fertile breeding ground for crushes, this is also the place where you make the magic beans that pay the gas bill. So make sure that if you lose one, you don't end up losing the other. That would be a disaster for your confidence on more levels than you even want to contemplate.

WHO IS HE?

If you are new to a position, don't dive in with someone immediately; it could turn out that he is the office shag-hound and you might end up feeling very stupid when you finally get to know him. If it's right, he'll still be working two desks over from you in a few months' time. If he is the post boy and you are the MD, be careful that you don't get slapped with a sexual harassment suit; many a broken heart has flounced off to tell the powers that be all their wounded stories. By the same token, if your target is your boss, then he might want to make you conveniently disappear post-romance: hard to imagine in the fluffy pink love bubble you first feel, but there is an extra dynamic to this particular fluffiness. Also be real about your expectations: disappointed that a post boy's salary doesn't even match your expense account? The boss that screams at subordinates is likely to become all sugary smiles and foot rubs after six? I doubt it.

Take a look at IDEA 4, *Learn from the masters*, on using other people's techniques to catch your prey.

Try another idea...

CONDUCT YOURSELF ACCORDINGLY

Don't cover his computer screen in love notes, email pictures of yourself naked (those kids in IT *can* access your personal mail, whatever they say...) and don't use group discussions to bring up personal issues ('Oh, making everyone tea, are we? You can barely find the cups at home...'). Don't tell his assistant how he failed to call when he said he would or try and sneak a look at his diary. Most of us, and especially men, need some time out from our most intense personal relationships and you will need to be even more professional around them at work than normal, to keep the pressure down. This will also have the benefit of making you seem unavailable and tempting even if you are normally a clingy stalker in all your other relationships.

PREPARE FOR UPS AND DOWNS

People will accuse you of favouritism, excessive ambition, using up all the milk, anything you can think of (and plenty of things you won't have anticipated). Office romances can push a lot of other people's buttons so you just need to ride it out until the gossips have tired of it. Just don't fuel the fire by giving up your dates at the water cooler if you want your romance, and your reputation, to last.

'You've achieved success in your field when you don't know whether what you're doing is work or play.'
WARREN BEATTY

Defining idea...

165

How did it go?

Q **Hideous. I had a hot summer fling with a colleague (too many after-work drinks) and now he's cooled and I feel so awkward about having to sit four desks away from him. What do I do?**

A *Lucky you.*

Q **Er, excuse me, which part of hideous didn't you understand?**

A *Look, when relationships end we often don't get to resolve the issues that come up for us; the other person can become a figure of hate or adoration and this can stop us from moving on. This way, you are forced to ride out the horror until you find yourself in mid-chat with him about a report and realise you're not blushing/scowling/crying but just responding naturally. It's a good chance to be a grown-up. Plus, it might spur you on towards getting a revenge promotion... Nothing would be more pleasing than showing him your new business cards.*

39

Ex alert

You've met a great guy, he seems really into you and things are ticking along nicely. Well done...

Only one problem: a past affair of his just hangs around like the proverbial hideous smell.

The key here is to know your enemy. What kind of ex is she?

THE SAPPY EX

She is incapable of calling a mechanic or opening a jar of pickles. She isn't looking to get him back, but needs his support whilst she waits for another strong man to come and work out how to wire up her DVD player.

- *She makes him feel*: Great; men like to feel strong and needed and, yes, a bit superior at times.

- *You should*: Resist the temptation to bang her head in the fridge door or tell her to grow up. You should also not try and make her look pathetic by acting super-strong; he will feel you don't need him. As the two of you get closer she will

Here's an idea for you... **It can be incredibly tempting to ask your partner about his ex, but you are making a rod for your own back here. Every time you feel the need to ask something, give yourself a little mental slap in the face: a little question asked innocently now is just something to torture yourself with later. Many a sleepless night has been spent trying to analyse the words 'Yep, she was pretty.' At the end of the day, exes are exes for a reason.**

naturally fade away as the idea of getting out of your warm bed to change her tyre in the rain gets old.

THE BITCHY EX

She either wants him back and can't help venting her frustration or she is basically just a common or garden bitch. She asks if your top is from a supermarket chain when it is clearly designer label, compliments you on being creative with such hard-to-manage hair and shrieks at his jokes like she is on laughing gas.

- *She makes him feel*: Desired. Only a woman who has forgotten to take her medication can laugh like that at every weak pun.

- *You should*: Never try to out-bitch. He won't see her veiled barbs for what they are, if she is making him feel good. If you smile sweetly, she may have to get so mean that even the most thick-skinned man (and they really are) will get the point. She wants a fight so don't give her one, and eventually she'll find fresh blood. He will also see for himself that he is just one member of her admirer harem and get bored.

THE DESPERATE EX

She wants him back, and bad. She sends him texts, remembers his birthday and sends handmade cards, has 'forgotten' to take his picture out of her wallet.

Working on your own confidence can be a great way to slay the ex demons; take a look at IDEA 51, *Real confidence.*

Try another idea...

■ *She makes him feel*: Guilty. He still meets up to make sure she hasn't thrown herself off a high building and assuage his own conscience.

■ *You should*: Make a united front, for all concerned. She needs to see he has moved on and that, as a result, so should she. Try and show compassion; we've all been there.

THE BEST PAL EX

Oh, she's a hoot, this one. She was his first love, they lost their virginity together, have loads of in-jokes, she laughs that he is her 'plan b' backup should she not meet the man of her dreams. She has a photo of them Inter-railing stuck to the door of her fridge.

■ *She makes him feel*: Safe. Like a sister.

■ *You should*: See it for what it is. It's incredibly annoying to have someone's closeness shoved in your face all the time but if they

'Living well is the best revenge.'
GEORGE HERBERT, English poet

Defining idea...

are still so matey, the chances are that the spark left ages ago. Concentrate on making your own memories with him to stick on your fridge, and she will probably realise she is being a bit tragic. Only time, and becoming more established as a couple, will make you feel better about this one.

HOW TO COPE

It can be soul-destroying to watch your man with his ex, especially if she is wrapping herself around him like a cheap suit. But there are some things you must try and avoid doing to keep yourself sane. Don't slag her off; he will end up defending her and that will push them together as a unit, rather than you and him. If you must bring something up, like her asking how long you had been growing your moustache, put it in context. Tell him that he knows her better than you and ask if she might have meant it as a joke, as you feel a bit awkward. That will get him ticking it over in his brain; he'll be more likely to notice other snipes. Try to avoid giving him an ultimatum; their relationship will cool as time wears on and if it doesn't, or she is incredibly hostile and he is unwilling to acknowledge her behaviour, maybe you should move on. He may never do so.

Q   **My boyfriend's ex is an arch-bitch. She is always calling him. He says she was a nightmare when they were together but he doesn't tell her to back off. What's going on?**

How did it go?

A   *He may be getting something from her that he doesn't get from you.*

Q   **Cheers! Like what?**

A   *What do you think it is?*

Q   **Well, she is always in contact but I have a demanding job and haven't got time to mess about. Could it be that?**

A   *It's about getting an ego massage, then. Let her get on with it; men might enjoy the attention of a high-maintenance woman like her, but they are rarely chosen as the mothers of their children.*

Q   **So, what, I just sit back?**

A   *Yes. She'll slip up at some point and show her neurotic colours, and he'll soon get tired of the demands.*

40

Be good to your mates

Sometimes things can be so great in our lives that we forget how hard we fought for them. Friends are one example.

The love of a good friend is like having emotional money in the bank; just make sure you take enough interest.

Good friends take years to cultivate: remember your best friend from when you were six? No, neither do I, but I do know that the crop of bosom buddies I have around me now has taken years to grow. Each is wildly different from the next and all give me some kind of support particular to themselves. But when this part of your life has been established for a while and the desire to meet someone great is uppermost in your mind, it is incredibly easy to forget that these relationships take maintenance too.

THE HUNT

Getting ready to go out with a friend is one of the great fun things about being a woman. But sometimes the booze starts flowing and suddenly you are the toast of the town and every Tom, Dick and their brother Barry wants to chat to you. Wonderful, this means you have avoided the single girl's bad habit of holing up in

Here's an idea for you... **From the start, create a Thursday night (or whatever night, of course) amnesty, where you *both* meet up with your mates. This will improve both sets of relationships; your friends will feel valued and you and your new man get the chance to miss each other.**

the corner of the bar bemoaning your fate and ignoring everyone else. But you must not, under any circumstances, leave your friend to count the knots in the leg of her wooden chair whilst you wax lyrical for hours on end. You may be out on the pull (and it's worth discussing how you handle this before you even get out of the taxi) but there is no reason why you can't all chat together. This has several advantages: no one ends up sitting there feeling awful, waiting to go home and sob about being the 'ugly one'; you show that you are a considerate person with more than sex on your mind; you can find out what kind of man he is. A decent one will be able to communicate his interest whilst still being polite. If you like him, consider setting a limit of no more than fifteen minutes and then give him your number and suggest that you reconvene at a more convenient time. This makes you seem very desirable, as you look like a woman in no way desperate and completely capable of entertaining herself, and it also stops you going home with a totally inappropriate man.

NOT BINNING HER OFF FOR HOLIDAY SEX

This one speaks for itself. If your friend has travelled seas and continents, spent precious time and holiday money, the last thing you should do is leave her on her own while you follow a local waiter around. You may think that she should understand that this is something special, but changing the rules once you have touched down is totally selfish. Date by all means, but beware: a week of fun in the sun isn't worth losing a good friend for, especially if you find that no one ever wants to holiday with you again when they hear about your antics.

MAKING TIME WHEN YOU MEET SOMEONE

Good friends understand the love-bubble effect; it usually lasts about three months and you may as well be glued into your home, because that's where you and your fling can always be found. But even when you are in this stage, make sure you call and keep up with their lives, make time to catch up. And once you are out of the bubble, make sure you set aside a regular time to keep in touch with your crew, or you may find yourself knee-deep in nappies at some point and wonder what happened to the old you.

IDEA 3, *Where do you meet a straight single man in this place, anyway?* will help your friend find her own playmate.

Try another idea...

LOOKING AFTER A SINGLE FRIEND

If you have been palling around town with a particular single friend for some time, she may find it a shock to the system that you are no longer available. You may end up arguing about silly things or she might call less and, easy though it is to feel self-righteous ('Why can't she just be pleased for me?'), you have to realise that your life has moved forward, while hers is still the same, but without you in it to the same degree. Make sure that you don't trivialise her fears about meeting the right guy or become impatient. Change makes everyone jumpy for a little while.

'Friendship is certainly the finest balm for the pangs of disappointed love.'
JANE AUSTEN, *Northanger Abbey*

Defining idea...

175

SMUG ALERT

Agh. The most frightening of all the transformations. Like ex smokers, born-again singletons who are now happily ensconced in a couple can be amazingly irritating. In your new state of bliss it's easy to erase the memory of all the disastrous dates you had and imagine that being single is the fault of the single friend. Sometimes it is, sometimes it isn't, but unless you want to become ostracised by all you know, button your lip – or they might be rubbing their hands with glee if you hit a rocky patch. And they'd be right to do so.

How did it go?

Q   My friend is being really strange with me about my new boyfriend. She is really critical. What's happening?

A   Do you think she is jealous?

Q   Possibly; we were thick as thieves before. Always slagging off men and glugging wine. What do you think?

A   Just by being in a relationship you are challenging her ideas about what is possible; she may have to stop moaning and start acting to find someone of her own. Let her know clearly that slagging him off is unacceptable, but you would love for her to meet someone too, and plan a date to get her out of her rut – one that actually involves being nice to men.

41

Be the popular girl

Meeting someone is often a numbers game: the more people you meet, the more likely you are to meet someone that you click with.

And the key to meeting someone you like is to get invited to everything, everywhere. And the key to being invited everywhere, is to be the best possible invitee.

GET A PLASTIC HEAD

This isn't as mad as it sounds, honest. Some days you really don't want to go out: the toast got burnt, you lost the cat, you were late for your pay review at work. But sometimes these are the days when you must summon every last bit of self-love and force yourself to turn up, even if you only stay for half an hour. This is for two main reasons. Whoever is throwing the do will be worried about the turnout, and even if you are a ship passing through, they will appreciate the effort, and remember it next time the invites go out (when you might be more in the mood). Secondly, you never know who might be there: Mr Correct could be nursing a warm beer looking for someone to talk to, and it might be six years until the universe throws him into your path again. Have your own 'plastic head': a face, or rather a state of mind that

Here's an idea for you... **Throw your own party. People are often motivated by self interest; thinking that they might get an invite to your bash in return might garner you a few more invites landing on the mat.**

sees you through – it should consist of a winning smile. If you still hate being there, give yourself permission to go home after half an hour. It's like the social version of the gym; you will feel better for making the effort no matter how much you didn't want to go.

GET YOUR TIMING RIGHT

Make sure that you know the right protocol for the right do. If it's a house party, you can expect it to be pretty flexible; a surprise party will need you to be on time and there before the guest of honour. Only ever arrive fifteen minutes either side of a dinner party invite; you don't want to find your hostess in a pinny or willing to strangle you with one because your tardiness has caused the roast lamb to burn. If you are going on your own, it is reasonable not to want to be the first to arrive, but don't roll in an hour after you should have got there; you may find yourself ostracised as people have settled into groups.

MAKE SURE YOU'RE SEEN

What's the point in making all that effort if no one sees you? Make sure you say hello to your host (and a grateful goodbye as you leave). Don't head over to people you know and skulk behind the coats. Pretend you are a shark: keep moving or you'll die.

GOOD MANNERS

Never take someone along with you unless directly asked to do so; if you really must take someone, make sure you confirm that this is fine beforehand. Make sure you RSVP in the way they requested; don't text 'yes' to a wedding if they wanted a reply card – it might be hard for them to keep track of, as well as everything else. Don't get so drunk that your hosts find you behind the sofa the next morning, don't insist they play another round of charades if they are parents and need to get up the next day.

Take a look at IDEA 12, *Being lucky at getting lucky*, on how to be ready for action when opportunities arise.

Try another idea...

SHOW YOUR APPRECIATION

Never turn up to an event which has a specific celebratory purpose empty-handed, even if you have been invited by a third party. Take wine at least, and always drop your hosts a line or give a quick call to say thanks.

TAKE THE PRESSURE OFF

Your hosts will probably be worn down to their very last nerve, so if you can help things go with a swing they will be eternally grateful. Don't just sit there staring into space; introduce yourself and introduce people you've just met to each other; ask questions – people always love to talk about themselves and will remember you as fascinating, even if you didn't say more than your name before you stepped aside for their monologue.

BEING POPULAR ISN'T THE SAME AS PULLING

You might be hoping that you'll meet someone, but some events are just about widening your social network, which means you might meet more people through those

'A good listener is not only popular everywhere, but after a while he gets to know something.'
WILSON MIZNER, US screenwriter

Defining idea...

179

people, and so it goes on. As a result, you don't need to turn up to every event looking like a Vegas showgirl who could only afford half the costume. If you do get invited to a fancy-dress party, don't always immediately assume it's a great chance to dress in something super-vampy; sometimes turning up dressed as a peanut is more winning and more people might chat to you, thinking you have a good sense of humour, rather than that you are looking to nail a man.

How did it go?

Q   **So, I went to a works party and actually went on time rather than getting drunk with the girls from the office beforehand. Impressed?**

A   *Yes. And how did that work out for you?*

Q   **Well I met some people who were just dropping in for early drinks before moving on, rather than just the drunken hangers-on at the end. I didn't hide behind a girl posse so had to actually speak to people sober. Was that better?**

A   *I think so. Any man action?*

Q   **A little, but I made a good work contact from another company. That's OK too, isn't it?**

A   *Certainly is. A new job can be great for the confidence boost, which can give you a booty confidence boost; and of course, who knows who could be lurking in the stationery cupboard at your next place of work...*

42

Get your life back

Too busy to find love? It's a common complaint. But it's easy to let work become disproportionately important.

Do you have a problem? Here's some help.

Work gives us an immediate satisfaction, and is also a financial necessity. Unless you are going to stay at your parents' house, wearing homemade dresses cut out of old curtains, until your husband gets delivered by post, you may need to earn your own crust. And even then, the reality is, most homes need two incomes to have a decent standard of living.

First of all, you need to work out how much of a change you need to make. You also need to know who is putting on the screws: do you have a demanding boss who makes you feel guilty for even going to the toilet, who is determined to buy a bigger house off the back of your commission? Or do you always offer to be the one to take up the slack?

BIG BAD BOSS

If it's the first of those two scenarios then you need to do some boundary resetting. Before you roll your eyes and stop reading, thinking you don't have any choices, you have to stop being so defeatist. People often do these things because they can. So take the power back. Learn to say 'no' and 'maybe'.

Here's an idea for you... **You could also use your work diary to identify which part of your job you really like, and see if you can do more of this and less of the other stuff. Why not? It's just as easy to make several changes at one time as it is to make one.**

If your boss is always asking you to do extra things, put the onus back on to them by saying that you can't possibly accommodate all the extra work and asking what they might suggest as a way of resolving that, as your manager. That is, after all, their job: to manage the work flow. You could even suggest freelance help, although you may need to work up to saying something a little pushier like that. When you do say no, then do it with a smile and be firm. Don't do it with a scowl, badly masking your anger, or you might find yourself in a very confrontational situation. But, more often than you would ever imagine possible, they will simply nod and take it to someone else.

As for the 'maybe': sometimes you will need to take on extra work relating to your particular skills or time pressure, but remember to negotiate. If you are working late or weekends to make this happen, make sure you let them know you are doing it as a favour – and that when you want to leave an hour early next Friday it's in exchange for this time. You need to stop feeling that you are always in debt to them.

BIG BAD YOU

Surprisingly, no matter how much you complain, you may be the reason you are at work till all hours. Maybe you are dreading going home to an empty flat or have convinced yourself that the office can't function without you. Maybe you work late to kill time until you meet friends.

WHAT IS WORK ANYWAY?

Take a look at IDEA 41, *Be the popular girl*, for ways to spend that free time effectively.

Try another idea...

It has been reported that people can spend up to four hours in a regular working day checking emails, making personal appointments and nattering on the phone. Find out what your productivity actually is, rather than what you think it is, by keeping a work detox diary (like a food diary). Every time you get up from your desk, write down the time and the activity; and include any time doing personal things at your desk. Once you have done a regular week, see where you could shave off any time, but also where you seem to have any patterns. Do you find yourself changing the coffee filters at midday? Most people have a natural energy lull around this time, which can be exacerbated by eating a carbohydrate-based lunch, inducing drowsiness. Look at the tasks you need to achieve; perhaps that report is best written in the morning whilst you are feeling peppy, and the photocopying done in your after-lunch lull.

Designate a lunch hour at the beginning of your week to do all the life-maintenance stuff such as paying bills or checking your bank balance. It will save you time but also help you create order in the rest of your life, too. If you find it hard to structure your work, set the alarm on your phone to hourly intervals, at which point you start your next task.

If you meet friends after work see if there is something more stretching you can do than sitting at your desk while you wait, such as a trip to the gym or an evening class.

'I don't want to achieve immortality through my work... I want to achieve it through not dying.'
WOODY ALLEN

Defining idea...

185

How did it go?

Q **Nice idea, but my boss is an unreasonable person with no private life and doesn't want any of us to have one. Wouldn't I be shooting myself in the foot?**

A *OK, I get that. If you can prove you've completed your work, you are legally entitled to leave. Start leaving on time and make a point of saying goodbye so that you don't look, or feel, like you are sloping off.*

Q **But what if I get sacked?**

A *There is enough legislation out there to make sure that can't happen, but if you are really worried, keep a diary of your hours and the work produced. Do you really want to be working for the same horror in a few years' time? Exactly; fight for your rights and get a life.*

43

Contraception choices

OK, so dating doesn't necessarily mean getting frisky, but let's face it: at some point, it usually does.

And with sexually transmitted diseases (STDs) on the rise, you need to think ahead and not get caught with your pants down (if you will excuse the phrase)...

MAKING AN INFORMED CHOICE

Safe sex has three simple contraception choices: condoms, condoms and condoms. No matter what other choices you have made, only this barrier method will offer you complete safety from STDs as well as pregnancy. Of course, they can rip and put you at risk, so you may want to also use another method of protection against pregnancy. Make it clear to a new beau that you are like the best VIP lounge in town; he can't get in without a jacket. If he can't accept those terms, he's probably not worth the invite.

KNOW THYSELF

Of course, every now and again we all have a sweet sherry too many and make a bad decision. If you frequently fall into this category (which I hope you don't) or would prefer some extra, stress-free protection against pregnancy, there are

Here's an idea for you... **Even if you think you know what has always worked for you, visit a family planning centre when considering a new (and hopefully) long-term contraception solution. New products enter the market all the time and you may be surprised at the experts' suggestions – even if it's just finding you a new pill that doesn't cause you to gain weight.**

methods that can take care of your fertility even when you don't. These include implants, some IUDs (intrauterine devices, or 'coils' as they are sometimes known) and the injection. Remember, however, all of these offer protection against pregnancy – not disease.

STICKING TOGETHER

Once you have moved into the realm of 'couple' you may want to lose the condoms. The pill is still a hugely popular choice for many women, with new brands entering the market all the time, with an ever more refined balance of hormones, so if you have problems with one type, try again and you may get much better results. Another great solution, and less permanent than their implant sisters, are hormone patches.

Right, now: let's look at those STDs in a bit more detail. Don't just stop reading – know your enemy...

WHAT'S TO FEAR?

The list of possible infections is daunting: HIV, herpes complex, candida, gonorrhoea, chlamydia, syphilis, hepatitis B... and certainly frightening. If that's still a bit of an abstraction for you, consider this: one million people around the world are infected with something sexually transmitted, every single day of the year.

Symptoms that can indicate an STD or STI (sexually transmitted infection) include soreness around the genitals or anus, which could be a rash, lumps and bumps, itchiness, or an unusual odour or discharge, and if you are

Take a look at IDEA 26, *When to do the deed*, on deciding when to take the plunge with a new man.

Try another idea...

concerned you should consult your doctor or visit a sexual health clinic. Although the clinic might seem like an embarrassing option, your doctor doesn't have to know the results of your tests: so if your GP has known you since you were five and plays cards with your gran, and you want to be tested, you might find it a good option. These clinics deal specifically with sexual health matters so are unlikely to be shocked or appalled at your arrival. At a clinic, they can also test for everything at once; they won't, however, test for HIV unless you ask them to. They will also be able to give you access to a counsellor should you want to talk through any fears or concerns you might have. Your local health centre will have a list of nearby facilities.

WHAT IF IT'S BAD NEWS?

Firstly, don't panic. Lots of STDs are easy to treat and leave no permanent damage. You will need to talk to your partner, though, about this

'*I'm too shy to express my sexual needs except over the phone to people I don't know.*'
GARY SHANDLING, US comedian

Defining idea...

news; if you are currently single and having a random check up, the clinic can contact anyone you think may have been at risk of infection on your behalf, and do so anonymously if necessary. If you are in an ongoing relationship, you must have your partner screened or you could pass it between the two of you indefinitely.

BRINGING UP THE BIG ISSUES

If you think you may be with a partner for any length of time, you may want to ask them to get tested anyway. Might seem like a truly mortifying thing to have to do, but at this stage he is likely to have seen you naked and with morning breath. You should, as a result, be able to bring this issue up with him; having contracted, or risked contracting, an STD is a pretty common occurrence and pretending that these things only happen to other people is the equivalent of thinking that the moon is made of cheese. You can always say that you would like to get tested so you can try an alternative method to condoms. The idea of riding bareback (i.e. without condoms) will quickly encourage him to make the smart choice, but on the understanding that he has the test too.

How did it go?

Q **I slept with a guy and the condom ripped; now I am obsessed with the idea that I'm pregnant. What can I do?**

A *Calm down. When did it happen?*

Q **Last night. It's too late, right?**

A *Don't panic. Firstly, you can take the morning-after pill which can prevent a pregnancy from developing further – but you only have seventy-two hours from the time of the 'accident' to do this. Another thing you should know is that it is not always effective, and the chances of it being effective reduce the longer you leave it, so do take it as soon as you can. As for the chances of infection, you might want to consider being tested as some infections, like chlamydia, can have few or no symptoms and result in infertility.*

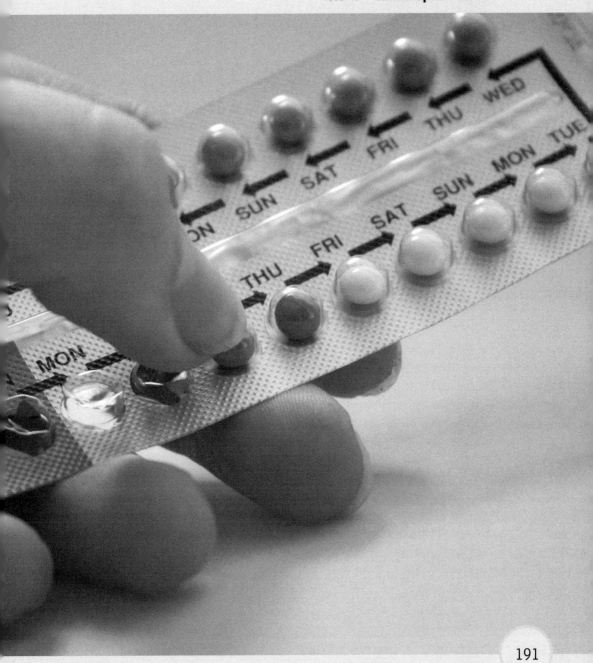

44

Live sexy

Picture the scene: you are having lunch by yourself in a quiet café; you look up and see two men at nearby tables. Both are nice looking, of equal build, and both keep looking at you...

The first, with unkempt hair and his collar all over the place, has his shoulders hunched over and flicks his eyes furtively at you from behind his paper.

The second sits back in his chair with his legs lightly crossed at the ankle, body faced towards you; he's casually dressed but in a well-cared-for way, waits for you to look up and gives you a slowly spreading wide smile before looking back to his menu. Which one appeals?

Of course you know nothing about either of them, but the guy who seems in a happy, self-possessed place is always going to be more of a draw than the one who looks like he needs to be put through a spin cycle on extra hot. And it's not all about body language; it's about the fact that we would all like to be with someone who can enrich our lives rather than drain them.

So here's a guide to making your life utterly desirable. Being wanted is always much more attractive than being needed.

Here's an idea for you... **Be the Mother of Invention. A common complaint from women is that men stop surprising them or whisking them away for treats and fancy weekends, but why shouldn't they expect the same in return? Keep coming up with new ideas for things for you both to try (skiing, badminton, naked horse-trekking in Peru...).**

The key to this is possession. Men want this. Not of you, but you having some possession of yourself. Your own life, your own friends, interests which a man can share and learn from. Only odd men and children want the women in their lives to be constantly at their beck and call. Other people need a partner who has more going for them than the fact that they have embroidered their initials on matching T-shirts.

I'M GREAT, I AM

Act like you know your own worth, even when you feel at a low ebb. Don't treat yourself like an old loaf of bread that should be marked down and be lucky to get turned into toast. Let someone feel that you like yourself and your virtues; this usually means turning off the self-deprecating drivel ('Oh no, I'm only the CEO because no one else wanted the job...').

NETWORKS

Friends are an essential part of a healthy woman's life. You can tell them stuff you don't want to worry your parents with, you can ask them if you look like a truck in that dress and get an honest answer, and they can help you drink/laugh/rage your way through misery. Having mates also lets a man know that you are socially adept, and are able to ask others for support rather than just him. No one wants a twenty-four-hour limpet relying on them for constant love and stimulus, unless they are a rock. Or just plain freaky.

FINANCIAL SMARTS

Understanding money and how to make the most of it is a great way to give yourself confidence; it's also a very attractive quality in another person. Make it your responsibility to understand how these things work rather than looking to him to bail you out. It will give you a great sense of well-being and security too: what's not to love?

Take a look at IDEA 51, *Real confidence*, for ways to build your self-esteem and help you get the life you want.

Try another idea...

HOME LIFE

Out every night of the week but come home to some kind of cesspit? Unless you are still a student, finding out that your potential new partner lives like a slob is not especially charming. Take some pride in your environment and see its knock-on effect on everything you do, from arriving at work early because you can actually find the matching parts of a suit or just being happy to spend time on your own because you can curl up in your nice comfy bedroom with some tea and the newspapers.

PLAYING OUT

Don't ask him to every single thing you do, so that he doesn't start taking your company for granted. Have weekends away with friends, girls' nights only and keep up your yoga class; these were all part of the reason he was interested in you in the first place (especially the yoga positions) so give them up now and you may both be left wondering what happened to the old, interesting you.

'I was always looking outside myself for strength and confidence, but it comes from within. It is there all the time.'
ANNA FREUD, Austrian psychoanalyst and psychologist

Defining idea...

195

How did it go?

Q **So I followed your advice and put my house in order and now I don't even think I want a boyfriend. Is this right?**

A *Hurrah. Then there will be one about to hit your life any time now.*

Q **Well, I think that makes sense. Does it?**

A *Of course. Looking for someone to fill a void inside you is a disaster for you both; people can sense it and stay away. Learning how to fill the void yourself means that people are drawn by all your feel-good energy and, if you are happy on your own, you are in the best position possible to meet Mr Right.*

Q **How's that?**

A *Because you will only want to share with someone truly worthy; the losers you would have sat by the phone waiting for before, suddenly seem total wastes of space.*

Q **So Mr Right will only come along when I'm past caring?**

A *I know, funny isn't it? Hasn't the universe got a naughty sense of humour?*

45

Is this it?

Well, doesn't life just kick you in the teeth sometimes? You got what you wanted and you're still not happy.

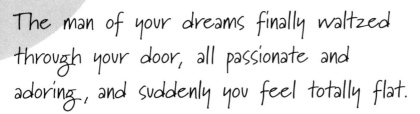
The man of your dreams finally waltzed through your door, all passionate and adoring, and suddenly you feel totally flat.

Everything he does from leaving love missives on your pillow ('What a waste of paper') to his constant cuddling ('Get off, you're smothering me!') drives you insane with frustration.

WHAT'S WRONG?

Chances are, not much. The reality is that after a long time alone you can become used to your own way of doing things. That's not to say that you are now the Wild Woman of Wonga, happier in the company of cats than other humans, but you will probably need an adjustment period. This might seem strange after you have spent some nights so desperate to meet the right guy that you were willing to reconsider the postman if only he would shave his back and stop wearing primary colours, but the heart is a funny old thing. If you have taken pleasure and comfort in treating yourself to a relaxed breakfast of fresh coffee and a granary muffin, you may

Here's an idea for you... **Avoid sofa rot at all costs. Once you have someone to share your down time with, getting out of your cosy jogging bottoms and over to see a friend on a drizzly night can seem like madness – but, at the risk of sounding like your mother, you'll enjoy it when you get there. You will feel a sense of accomplishment when you get home; you've not had your whole evening swallowed up by watching DVDs and there'll be a little soul glow from nurturing a connection with a friend. It also gives both you and your partner the time to miss each other. Make a commitment to yourself to try and ensure this happens at least once a week.**

become resentful if he fries an egg and shoves it between two Weetabix as he runs out through the door, leaving you the oily mess.

THE BIG C

The big C in any relationship is not always commitment, but change. You have to be willing to let some of the good things go as well as the bad. Goodbye loneliness, bored Sunday nights and Christmases with your gran busy trying to find out if you're a lesbian, yes, but also goodbye to only having to do the washing once a week and lying starfish-shaped in the bed, or calling your best friend and watching a film together over the phone. You will naturally resist giving those things up.

ALL BY MYSELF

The most confusing emotion that can arise from being in a relationship is that of isolation. You may find yourself turned off at the idea of joining the girls in an endless round of drinks when it seemed to be great fun before. That might be because your objective (to pull) and the conversation (pulling) are less relevant. You need to find new ways to play.

Make sure you keep hold of what's important; take a look at IDEA 44, *Live sexy*, on having an enviable life.

Try another idea...

THE PHONE STOPS RINGING

You used to spend all your time waiting for him to call, now you're desperate to hear the voice of one of your friends inviting you out. If you have let things slide, make the first call. Organise something and even be prepared for a little resentment to come your way; feelings might be a bit bruised but having a phone stand-off and your own little pity party won't make them fade. Be constructive; have a real party instead and remind everyone how much fun you are.

NOT ALL ABOUT THE BOY

Some changes are purely about entering a new phase of your own life. You might quite easily have been ready for change regardless of meeting a new person, so you may need different challenges to make you feel engaged. It is often the case that when we meet someone we throw all our energy into that relationship, with work and friendships taking a back seat. When we emerge from the three-month fog (that's its usual duration), we might find ourselves realising we don't want to pick up where we left off. Naturally you will have less time available, so being your sister's on-call babysitter might not work for you any more if you still want to catch up with the girls; ditto schlepping across town to visit that old friend who only wants to see you to whine about her husband.

'Happiness is not achieved by the conscious pursuit of happiness; it is generally the by-product of other activities.'
ALDOUS HUXLEY, British writer

Defining idea...

How did it go?

Q   I waited years to find Mr Right, and now he has turned out to be Mr 'I Haven't Got Time Right Now'. When we first got together he adored me; now I get the ratty moods at the end of his day at work. What went wrong?

A   *Nothing went wrong, real life just arrived. This is what happens when you move from wooing to serious; real life re-enters the frame and with it people start seeing their other dreams and ambitions needing attention.*

Q   **So now I'm just part of the furniture?**

A   *Only if you keep up your bad attitude. Want to reinstate those lovely chats you had when you were first together? Cook dinner, ban the TV and sit opposite each other at the table. Then stop talking and start asking: ask him about his day or what he feels like doing at the weekend. Pretty soon he'll start doing it in return (although it might take more than one meal). Once he doesn't feel challenged or criticised, he will start to look forward to coming back and may even come back early. If you want to be listened to, lead by example and listen.*

46

Falling too fast

It's a common complaint for men and women: but let's face it, mainly *about* women. You meet a guy, you have a couple of dates...

And before you know it, you've mentally picked a china pattern and are wondering how much of his stuff you'll need to get rid of before he moves in.

Yes, you find yourself crushing like a teenager and before you know it you're no longer gazing mistily into his eyes but at his back receding into the dust trail as he sprints away from you...

WHY AM I SO INSANE?

A lot of these over-eager and needy feelings come from the desire for intimacy, closeness and all your future dreams – but because he's the focus for them, it is easy to imagine that if he goes, your world will fall apart too. As long as you know where these feelings come from, you have a chance of controlling them.

Here's an idea for you... **If you have a hard time controlling yourself, write a list of the things you end up doing (baking him cakes, doing his washing, walking his dog...) and, like a junkie, allow yourself only small doses. Allow yourself one 'good deed' a week and stick to it.**

WHAT YOU WANT ISN'T ALWAYS WHAT THEY WANT

When you meet someone you like, with whom you think there might be some serious potential, you will want to show them you care. You would love to get a sign from them that they are interested, so you think that's what they want too. So you call, email and text; send a little loving note or buy them a gift. OK, so far, not so bad. But then you start rearranging your other plans to be available for them, you offer to drop off their dry cleaning. All of this is a well-intentioned attempt at wanting to make their lives easier. But pretty soon the balance tips in their favour and you have become their own personal maid.

It won't be long before this starts to destroy your relationship, closely followed by your sense of self-worth. The reason being so nice can have such disastrous effects is that you haven't given love the chance to bloom. You've squashed any chance of feelings evolving in their own right, and everyone needs to feel that they have chosen their partner themselves, rather than that they were bought, flattered or fed into being your lover. As well as them now feeling smothered, you will also start feeling resentful that they never seem to match your level of commitment or consideration.

You also run the danger of setting the bar too high. If you are always cooking for men, giving them gifts and having their mates lounging over your sofa while you serve them beers as they watch the match on your widescreen TV, what are you going to do for an encore? How on earth do you treat them on their birthday? World cruise? Before you know it, being the full-time perfect girlfriend will mean you have to give up your job, friends and sanity: if you let your levels drop they'll only think you've gone cold...

IDEA 21, *Why men love bitches*, will give you some ideas on how to release the bitch in you.

Try another idea...

The biggest danger is that you won't be able to do anything with any peace of mind unless you are getting their approval, and no one should have that much power over you. You might also realise, as the neediness balances out, that this particular man was not actually suitable for more than a fling – and now you have to extricate yourself from a situation after all your over-eager, hollow promises.

HOW TO LEARN TO PACE YOURSELF

Don't worry. If you are cringing with embarrassment at this point, give yourself a break; most people have slipped into this behaviour at some stage. It just needs a little self-control and a few mind tricks to stop you from falling into old habits. Now think of yourself as an expensive wine; give your next man too much, too soon and you'll make him drunk with excitement, a bit unsteady on his feet, and then eventually sick at the very sniff of you. Dole out your loving nectar in well measured portions. You need to give him the chance to savour every mouthful, and be excited about anticipating the next. Be aware that anything that comes too easy doesn't seem valuable: if you want to be treated like a princess, don't act like a kitchen porter. If you don't give him the chance to do nice things for you, he won't get to feel that soppy glow as well.

'Speak the truth, but leave immediately after.'
Slovenian proverb

Defining idea...

How did it go?

Q **Agghh! I'm horrified; you have just described my last four relationships and I think I've just done it to the latest. What do I do?**

A *Congratulations; welcome to sanity land. Now you know where you have been going wrong you can change your fortunes. It's not necessarily too late for your current beau.*

Q **How do I salvage things after having said the 'L' word in the first month?**

A *Hmm. Well, if he's still calling, he must think you have some qualities worth hanging in for – or he may just realise he's on to a good thing. (Bear in mind that even if a guy is nice, he might not see you as a serious proposal and still have you around if he's having to do his own shopping.) Try hanging back from making calls, be the first to end the phone conversation and make sure you aren't available for the next date he suggests; you need to establish some distance.*

Q **What if I've blown it?**

A *Then make a promise to yourself that this is the last one you over-love and move on. If you pointlessly berate yourself you will only be worse with the next one.*

47

How to make anyone want you

Die-hard romantics may want to look away now. Unless they really want to hook someone special...

Using a few tricks to get someone interested isn't just a cynical ploy. Real love will follow if it's right; this just gets you to the place to find out.

LOOK AT ME

What makes somebody feel attracted to one person rather than another? We all have a physical 'type' that we may respond to, but studies show that we also need to feel that we must have something in common with that person. This is why you might find people who dress similarly drawn to each other; there's an element of tribal recognition (yes, even amongst accountants). It makes us imagine that we may have shared values and interests. But there are also other ways that we are drawn together, too.

People in love often hold eye contact for longer than regular friends. To make the object of your affections start to feel that there may be something more between you than he had realised, hold his gaze. When you have to turn to talk to another person, make sure you hold his look a beat longer than normal and then drag your eyes reluctantly away. Even though you are doing the staring, you are simulating the actions of two people in love, and you will at least have him wondering.

MIRRORING

Mirroring is a technique that has been observed by psychologists in happy couples, in fact it seems to be essential to their happiness. They often finish each other's sentences or seem entirely in tune when performing tasks, such as cooking together or running the household schedule. The reason that couples feel so good together when this occurs is that both people feel that their needs and desires are being met and, most importantly, understood. The great news is that if you are looking to make an impact on someone, you can cheat this closeness and use it to get their attention. Good flirting uses this technique from the very start, in the form of sexy body language; touching your face if they touch theirs, leaning forward if they do... it seems to be a natural instinct that we can lose as relationships evolve and we get defensive. If you're feeling defensive in the first place, of course, you probably won't do this – so make a deliberate effort.

Here's an example. If you are attracted to someone at work and they are ranting away about the boss, leaning forward and bashing the table, then pulling back and leaning away from them would suggest that you feel dispassionate or detached from their experience, and make them feel uncomfortable or misunderstood. Not what you want to convey. Repeat back to them ideas or phrases that they use, or make comments such as 'I can understand why you feel frustrated' or 'I really sympathise with that'. This will make them feel as if you both share a common bond and world view, something essential to falling in love. Of course, we have all experienced the connection that turns out to be all surface and no content, but we are always drawn by that initial pull.

To see what sort of effect you are having, take a look at IDEA 11, *Is he interested?*

Try another idea...

DRAWING THE LINE

There is a difference between mirroring someone's behaviour and becoming a strange, puppet-like version of them. You can still disagree with them and take a different stance on things, but it is a good way of allowing someone to feel understood before you get into that sticky place where you disagree (which we are all bound to do at times). Think of how frustrated you would be if you got home from an annoying afternoon shopping with your mum and your man was lying on the sofa flicking through a newspaper: you'd at least want him to put it to one side and sit upright so you'd feel like you were getting his attention. If you have been together for a little while, and feel that things quickly seem to jump to a state of friction between the two of you, then try getting back to a place of complicity by employing this technique.

'Imagination is the beginning of creation. You imagine what you desire, you will what you imagine and at last you create what you will.'
GEORGE BERNARD SHAW

Defining idea...

207

How did it go?

Q **This all sounds very good, but it also sounds a bit dodgy. I want someone to fall in love with me because we are meant to be together, not because I'm playing tricks with their brain chemistry, don't I?**

A *Ah ha, we have a romantic.*

Q **So?**

A *Do you remember your first teenage love? Didn't you sit around and snog for hours and gaze into each other's eyes at the bus stop?*

A **Exactly. We were in love; properly in love. What's your point?**

Q *But you also, perhaps, hadn't been hurt before. A big problem for people finding love older than the age of sixteen, is the amount of self-consciousness and fear that comes up; what is being described here is returning back to the time when you were willing to open up and be exposed. Do you find it hard to make eye contact in bars or flirt?*

Q **A bit. OK, yes. And?**

A *If it's because you are embarrassed to not have your attraction returned, that's fear talking. Loosen up and give this a go; it's not a magic spell and won't work on someone who finds you repulsive, but it will make people feel drawn to you. Get over your Cinderella fantasies and get your act together. The rest, as they say, is down to chemistry...*

48

Green-eyed monsters

Ugh. Is there anything more hideous? Anything that makes you feel more uncomfortable or loathe yourself quite like jealousy does?

The bad thing is, it can kill off a budding relationship with the speed of a biblical-scale locust attack.

UNDERSTAND AND DISARM THE BOMB

Firstly, you need to work out what jealousy is and where it comes from. Because if you don't, you could start killing off your budding relationships for totally bizarre reasons. The worst thing that you can do is point your finger at the other person and blame them for your feelings (unless, of course, they are trying to wind you up), so repeat after me: I am bonkers. Once you acknowledge that questioning a perfectly reasonable person about their movements, outfits, phone calls and even a brief exchange with a waitress is the behaviour of a crackers person, you can start to get it under control.

Here's an idea for you...

Are they feeding the fire? Sometimes your intuition may actually be at work, and your partner may encourage advances to pep up his ego or keep you on your toes. Some relationships flourish on this added zip, some founder. If this is a genuine problem confront it early on and if he won't modify his behaviour, or you can't learn to see it as harmless ego-boosting, you may need to cut your losses. Or you could go insane.

FEELING SICK

This sensation initially seems to be about feeling that you know some hidden truth, when in reality it is more likely to be from insecurity, anger (at yourself) and self-loathing at being unable to control your jealous outbursts. Low self-esteem, feelings of insecurity, the fear of vulnerability or abandonment can all be causes for your reaction. Previous hurts from other relationships can make you so convinced that people are untrustworthy that you end up causing your current relationship to implode.

CHEMICAL REACTION

So how will all this affect your partner? Sometimes people get angry when questioned, which the jealous person can read as guilt. They can also feel undermined as you seem to be suggesting that they are unable to defend themselves from other people's advances – after all, they've managed to keep the creep who grins at them in the bus from moving in, so why should they have lost all interpersonal skills since you came along? The other person might start acting cold because they feel badgered – and so the cycle of anger and frustration begins. You should really try to stop trying to interpret their actions and remind yourself that they have their own way of dealing with things: just because they smile and then say a polite 'no, thanks' to someone's advance, where you would prefer them to ignore the person, doesn't mean they are wrong. The fact is that if you are feeling jealous they could probably karate-chop any potential suitors and you would still disagree with them having the physical contact.

Take a look at **IDEA 44, *Live sexy*,** on getting a desirable life that will give you confidence to help settle uncomfortable feelings.

Try another idea...

HOW TO STOP THE ROT

Firstly, be willing to apologise. If you manage to complete the initial step, which is not saying the jealous thing in the first place, you might find yourself holding back and being cold; this is just another way of punishing the other person. Take away the sting by saying, 'Look, I'm sorry, I've just had some totally ridiculous jealous thoughts and I am being a bit strange.' That gives the other person the chance to talk through your fears with you without feeling attacked.

Next, be willing to see jealousy as part of the fuller picture of a young relationship; if you have feelings for someone it is quite normal to feel possessive and curious, and to have a sense of ownership. You are also bound to feel vulnerable as you get closer to someone. And you also still have eyes in your head – spotting someone attractive in the street is going to happen, as will people fancying you. Unless you want to live in a dark wooden box in the middle of the forest, just the two of you, you should try and see it as a healthy part of life. Demonising it will only make you both feel frightened to open the door to the postman/woman.

Finally, you need to ask yourself why you feel that this is getting out of control. These feelings are always about yourself, so you need to think about engaging in some activities that aren't focused on the other person in the relationship.

'*Jealousy is all the fun you think they had.*'
ERICA JONG, US novelist, *Fear of Flying*

Defining idea...

Q **Things started out great between us, and now I feel very jealous of my boyfriend of four months. I feel so uncomfortable about the way I am behaving that I just feel like calling it off. Can you help?**

A *When did the feelings start?*

Q **About a month ago. And?**

A *Is he doing anything differently?*

Q **Spending a lot of time at work with his co-worker, a rather attractive blonde. But I am not normally such a weird, insecure person; what's wrong with me?**

A *Maybe you are experiencing possessiveness gone awry. Did you spend every waking hour together in your honeyed first three months?*

Q **Yes. Would that be it?**

A *Possibly – maybe you feel neglected and she is just an easy hook to hang your hat on; easier to blame her than accept that things have changed. Now you have re-entered reality he is paying attention to other priorities in his life, like work, which can seem like the popping of the love bubble. Talk to him about how much of his time you need; you might just need a bit more time together in order to feel special again.*

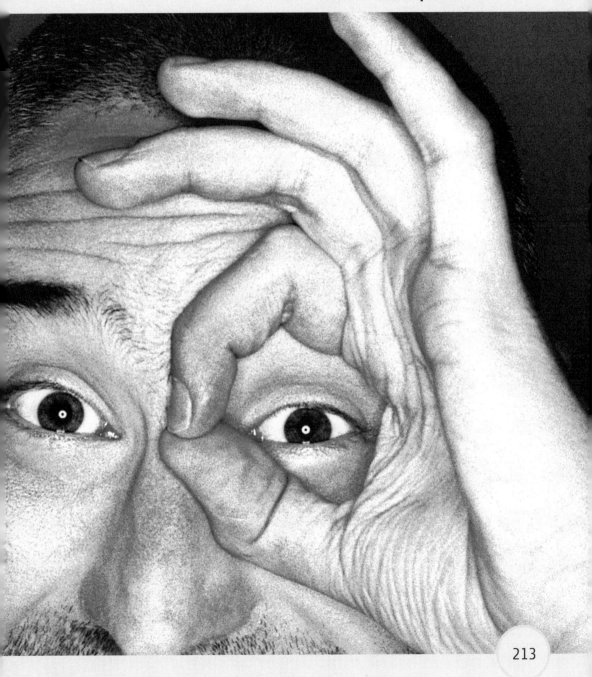

213

49

Is it ever right to go back?

Sometimes the wild and free land of singledom seems full of opportunity and wonder, with a veritable herd of possible lovers beating down your door.

Sometimes it's cold out there, only you and the cat rattling round your kitchen. That's when the most feared of all dating demons can rear its ugly head: the ex.

Of course, some relationships had rocky beginnings and went on to be great, enduring, stable loves; the push and pull of the splitting-up/back-together phase might have been the ex trying to come to terms with a fear of intimacy. But other ex-relationships just sap you of any remaining energy and stop you from moving on and finding a really meaningful connection. How do you know which one you are looking at?

EX SEX; THE EASIEST FIX

Hands up anyone who hasn't fallen into bed with an old flame. We've all told ourselves that we can handle it, it's just the comfort of a familiar shape in the bed,

Here's an idea for you... **Time to get the paper out. This exercise will really help you stop the ambivalence; if you are worried that you might not be really truthful because you are invested in a certain outcome, get a plain-talking friend round who won't be wearing the rose-tinted glasses and work through these questions. Did the relationship make you happy? What were the good and bad points? What could you have done better? Why did you break up (being too young is very different to being physically abused)? What would you like the relationship to be like if it was renewed? Are you, and is he, willing to work through any of the key issues to make that happen?**

someone to talk to who already understands your problems with your mother. And what do you know, you may even get through an evening without a single round of finger pointing. But there is a big difference between ex sex (which *does* have a cost, everything comes with a price) and a past relationship that can truly be rekindled. Ask yourself why you find yourself back in this space. Do you really want this person back? Or do you really just want *someone*? Do you have butterflies in your tummy because you had a great time together or are you just excited and flattered that they want you back?

I DON'T REMEMBER YOU

The biggest problem with returning to an old flame is that you are looking at it from a place of safety (although this can be a good thing, too). You may have become resilient, got over the knocks to your confidence that his constant barbs caused or forgotten how he used to jibe you about your weight. You have healed and forgotten the bad stuff, and as he's on his best behaviour, not his 'real', in-a-relationship-with-you behaviour, it can stay forgotten too. Another scary side of this is that your ex knows you well, so he may realise that telling you how great you look in that dress (something you would have killed to hear the first time around) is a great way to get under your skin. You might even be tricked into thinking he is your soulmate: wrong. He just knows where your buttons are and which ones to press. This isn't so much as a charm offensive as offensive charm.

Take a look at IDEA 14, _Putting the past where it belongs_, on how to move on.

Try another idea...

YOU CAN'T NOT KNOW WHAT YOU NOW KNOW

By now you may be running around the room in a blind panic totally confused, wondering if your ex is trying to screw you or screw with your mind. Relax. There are two vital elements in your favour when considering getting back with an ex. Firstly, you can't not know what you now know – which means you are in a better, more informed place than you were before: forewarned is forearmed. (And if you worry that you will be 'tricked' again, close the door straight away: unless he is a magician this is a very worrying sign.) Secondly, you have the power: if someone wants you back, you are in a position to make requests regarding intentions and behaviour. If you ask him if he still thinks spending four nights in the pub with his mates is reasonable (and you don't), and he tries to persuade you that you are just being possessive, say a polite thanks but no thanks; if he really wants you he will be expecting – and willing – to resolve the issues that broke you up. You may find it awkward asking the question but without communication this thing isn't going anywhere anyway. If you don't tackle this you may get hurt all over again but even more painfully, as this time around you are going to be angry at yourself for walking *yourself* into the same trap.

'Those who cannot remember the past are condemned to repeat it.'
GEORGE SANTAYANA, philosopher

Defining idea...

217

Q **Ah, I'm rubbish. My ex calls and I just keep running. He says he wants me back, but nothing ever seems to change. What can I do?**

A *Darling, he just wants you on your back. Next time he calls say you're available for coffee and see if he is willing to have a clothed, non-sexual date with you – then set out your rules for any future relationship. If he balks at the idea you will know for sure that he doesn't care; right now he's got his cake, is eating it and doesn't even have to pay for it.*

Q **But then I am totally alone, aren't I?**

A *Well, if that's your reason for hanging in there, you're as bad as he is; you need to overcome your fear and build a proper single life to nourish you. That way, when he puts in a booty call at 11 p.m. on a Friday the phone will just ring and ring... how good is that? Revenge and self-respect.*

50

Creating a romance lair

We spend over a third of our lifetimes in bed, and if we're lucky, we get to share a nice portion of that time with someone else.

But the chances of that are greatly reduced if we bring them home to reveal a stained mattress on the floor with an unwashed duvet and a pile of pizza boxes...

For both your sakes, apply some thought and make your bedroom beautiful.

SETTING THE SCENE

Before we even look at the main stage (that's the bed...) we need to create a tranquil and calm haven. A bedroom, space permitting, should be purely for sleeping, romancin' and reclining. All other activities such as watching TV, playing video games (you'd be surprised) and working should be taken elsewhere. Over-stuffed cupboards and drawers will also add to a sense of chaos and remind you that you haven't done the ironing; if you can, keep your clothes out of your sleep space but if that's not possible, make sure you put all your unseasonal wear (e.g. winter clothes in summer) into storage, so you have less to accommodate.

Here's an idea for you... **Sleeping is nature's stress reliever and making sure that you get at least six and a half hours a night will make you calmer, happier and more able to deal with emotional stress. The chemical that tells us we are ready to sleep, serotonin, is released as the day gets darker and tells our bodies to get sleepy. Even the red standby light on your TV can interfere with this, so put tape over it and get effective blinds or lined curtains to keep out street lights – the effect on your quality of sleep will be dramatic. If you find waking a miserable experience, get a sunlight alarm clock that mirrors the effect of dawn, gradually waking you up and letting you wake in a better mood.**

When choosing a colour to use to decorate your room, avoid anything over-stimulating such as bright orange or red, which is great for firing up the mind in the workplace but a disaster for taking you to a calm place at the end of a hectic day. Think restful colours such as a yellow-based white (not one based on blue, as this can look cold and hospital-like), an indulgent mocha or a sweet pale violet: all guaranteed to calm the soul. Make sure you also get rid of overflowing jewellery and make-up boxes, and declutter the surfaces; mess adds to a general feeling of chaos and, frankly ladies, if you are bringing home a prospective romance you want to say organised and peaceful, not tense, neurotic and living like a teenager.

GETTING THE RIGHT TOOLS

Now you have the right mood, you can make up the bed. The rule is, spend as much as you can afford. Not only will good bedding last you longer, but the benefits of a good night's sleep on your general well-being and productivity can't be overstated. Natural fibres are also the best option; they regulate the body temperature, take moisture away from the skin (should your nocturnal activities make you a little hot and bothered) and last far longer than man-made fibres. The luxury version for duvets is Siberian goose down (which would last between ten and fifteen years) but any feather ranges will give great comfort (and excellent support in pillows).

Take a look at IDEA 26, *When to do the deed*, on deciding on when to woo them back to your boudoir in the first place.

Try another idea...

But then, of course, is the pressing issue of what you put next to your skin – or rather someone else's. Despite the myth that black satin has wonderful aphrodisiac qualities (if you can manage not to slide off black satin sheets), linen is the kindest, and softest on the skin. For that boutique hotel level of luxury, look out for a high thread count (never less than 200) – the finer the weave, the more gentle on the skin.

If you are a sensitive soul and have allergies then always buy anti-allergenic, make sure you use the right detergent, and have your duvet and pillows dry cleaned frequently to get rid of dust mites. Curtains, padded headboards and carpets can also cause problems so get rid of them if you can.

MAKE ROOM FOR THE ACROBATICS

When looking to buy a bed, bear in mind that we move around sixty times a night (and that's sleeping only) and a standard double bed only gives you twenty-seven inches of sleeping space per person – less than a single bed! If you want a decent night's sleep splash out on a king-size bed; it will give you a lot more room to play with...

'Passion makes the world go round. Love just makes it a safer place.'
ICE T, US rapper

Defining idea...

Q **Yeah yeah, all very good but I'm a working woman with more things to do than fluff pillows and try to make my place look like a magazine. Now what?**

A *Well, I don't like your attitude but I see your point; it's better to admit that you are a slob and work round it.*

Q **Funny. So any quick tips?**

A *Get a bed with drawers under it that you don't use for storage; that way if you have created a bombsite getting ready to go out, you can fling everything in them and put things away properly when you have more time. Secondly, get cotton sheets that have been treated so that they are non-iron; a rumpled bed can look dirty even if it's clean. Get a linen spray or fragranced candle to set the mood; the sense of smell is incredibly evocative and can quietly scream seduction. And get a low-wattage lamp next to the bed; everything (and everyone) looks better in the semi-darkness.*

Real confidence

Often women carry their own worst enemy around: a lack of confidence. We can create unrealistic expectations and then use them to berate ourselves when things go wrong...

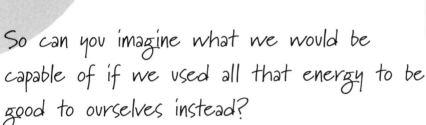

So can you imagine what we would be capable of if we used all that energy to be good to ourselves instead?

WHAT IS SELF-CONFIDENCE AND WHY DON'T I HAVE ANY?

Self-confident people trust their own abilities, talents, instincts and feel as though they have some control over the outcome of their lives. This does not mean that they think of themselves as invincible or faultless, but they do have a sense of achievement and self-worth. If they can't achieve one of their aims, they don't lose perspective and feel useless; a familiar feeling in those lacking in confidence. This is why someone lacking in confidence might be unwilling to try new things or make plans: the fear of stirring up those uncomfortable feelings is too great.

Sometimes being overly criticised in childhood, being bullied at school, or even some dramatic event can rock our confidence – which has nothing to do with our ability or the truth of who we are. We can then start to look to others for approval and esteem, making our core shaky and unstable, and we then become reliant on these 'fixes'. Everyone has a friend who needs the constant attention of men or runs

Here's an idea for you...

Next time, ask yourself who you would be without this fear and imagine how things would be different; it's a great way of exploding myths. So if you think, 'Who would I be if I went to the toilet when I needed it?' you could realise that answer is, 'Someone who doesn't hop around on the spot like a thing possessed'. It's a great way of realising how funny some fears are, and laughter is a great antidote to fear.

up credit card bills buying new clothes; these are classic examples of someone trying to 'make' confidence from elsewhere.

GET IN THE DRIVING SEAT

The main way we attack or own confidence is to collect 'facts' that support a negative idea, such as 'I'm so stupid, I failed my driving test just like I failed my Girl Guide cooking badge'. Hello? You were twelve! What about all the things you have succeeded at between now and then? Feelings aren't truth. We can imagine that a feeling holds some truth, but feeling unattractive and being unattractive are two different things; you need to learn to appreciate that sometimes feelings are just fears cropping up and not golden nuggets of insight.

Another major confidence-destroyer is the 'perfectionist' syndrome, the idea that if we can't be the best there is no point in trying. The best at what? Everything? An Olympic athlete might be the best at the high jump but can't dance; does that mean that her gold medal doesn't count? Confident people get failure and success in perspective – two sides of the same coin. There's nothing more charming than someone who admits with a smile that something isn't their forte.

ALL-TIME LOSERS!

So here are some of the most common things we tell ourselves that men don't like about us as women; the things we are adamant will have them running for the hills. This isn't to make you blush but to show you how confidence is all about giving only yourself the option to disprove of yourself and how to put a happy spin on stuff.

Take a look at IDEA 37, *Busting the bad days*, for some ideas on confidence-building actions you can take.

Try another idea...

- *Men love loud, sexy women.* True. Some men do love sassy women. But some loud women are attention-seeking energy drains: which is not the same as confident. And some quiet women are incredibly confident and don't feel any urge to run off their mouth and demand that they are the focus of everyone in the room. So forget focusing on her, and start paying attention to your own key assets.

- *I have to be gorgeous all the time.* According to whom? Most men are mildly, if at all, self-critical. Do you think that he imagines his slightly flabby love handles in any way affect his power as a love god? Trying to be immaculate all the time is more likely to make him think you are a vain android that doesn't sleep. Scary.

- *I'm a bit of a crackpot.* He either wants you or he doesn't. We all have our strange little habits, such as humming the *1812 Overture* when shaving our legs (for some of us it's a battle, OK?). It makes us different from the next person and all the more approachable. Don't try and second-guess what he wants from you; you are bound to get it wrong.

'Believe in yourself! Have faith in your abilities! Without a humble but reasonable confidence in your own powers you cannot be successful or happy.'
NORMAN VINCENT PEALE, US writer

Defining idea...

■ *I don't urinate.* When we feel out of control, we often try and take control. So we decide that if we start controlling aspects of our life we will be able to keep hold of the relationship. Insecurity comes from a fear of being rejected so we start obsessing about eradicating anything that might turn him off – and end up pretending we don't pee, like Barbie. Truth is, he'll do what he wants when he wants; you turning yourself into a human pretzel will just be exhausting for you both.

How did it go?

Q   OK... I thought I was quite confident then I realised I don't urinate. Does that mean I'm not?

A   *That's fine; we all have areas of confidence that need a little tweaking. Real confidence is about realism: just because you know you are great at your job it doesn't mean that you expect to be a great skier, right?*

Q   Exactly; I think I have a pretty good overview so why do I pretend not to pee?

A   *Because falling for someone new can bring up lots of old insecurities that need questioning, and then throwing aside. Next time this happens to you, laugh at your daft old self and then head for the bathroom...*

Are we there yet?

Prince Charming? Check. Hearts and flowers? Check. Relating to love songs on the radio? Check. Feel-good, mushy stuff? Check.

It all looks like it could be the real thing, but does it add up to it?

WHAT IS THIS STUFF YOU HUMANS CALL LOVE?

So, imagine this, you find an alien in your wardrobe and you are giving him a crash course on Planet Earth. How would you explain that strange and wonderful thing called love? Firstly, you might say that two individuals get drawn to each other; discover they have some things in common, some not; like to spend time together and then throw some happiness and desire into the mix for good measure. If things go well, it develops into being in love. At this point the alien might confuse it with madness.

When you are in love you think about the other person all the time, worry that they will never call you again, imagine that they are the funniest and smartest individual that ever lived. Then when real love rolls around – a less heady chemical mix but making up for it in substance – you start thinking long term, become willing to change your whole life to have more of the other person in it, and want the best for them and their well-being: to the point where yours depends upon it too.

Here's an idea for you...

So you think it's time to take things up a notch? Make sure you say 'I love you' in the best way possible, rather than blurting it out drunkenly because he gave you half his cheeseburger. Because, remember, once it's out there you can't go back.

BUT ARE WE *THERE* YET?

But of course, you might have the L word teetering on your lips but want to know if it's reciprocated before you blurt it out... Wise move, as saying it too early can squash a burgeoning relationship and make someone pull away. A few little checks will see if you have made it to the number one priority slot. (Don't worry, your prospect doesn't have to have achieved all of them...)

It's more than likely if the other person:

- Expects you to spend weekends together
- Runs plans by you for approval
- Wants you to meet his mum, dad, extended family, cat, fish, hamster...
- Assumes you will be spending your holidays together
- Remembers your favourite chocolate treat and brings one back with the Sunday papers
- Is willing to go out and get the Sunday papers
- Buys you gifts, in the right size
- Wants to treat you to nice dinners or save you cooking by arriving with a takeaway
- Will give you a foot rub and not always expect sex in return
- Will run you a bath when he knows you've had a hard day
- Knows if you are 'dieting' (don't mention the crisps you wolfed down)
- Will negotiate on what film to see
- Lets you choose the side of the bed you want

- Is your best friend
- Invites you to a close friend's summer wedding, and it's only December
- Comes across town to look after you when you are ill and will find an all-night chemist
- Sleeps better with you than apart
- Will talk finances without embarrassment and you know what he earns
- Saves things to tell you when he next sees you
- Gives you space in his bathroom cabinet
- Picks you up from the airport
- Doesn't care that Valentine's Day has gone all commercial but does something anyway
- Goes shopping with you for an important dress (but never make anyone do this too often; it's a giant favour…)
- Doesn't look terrified when you talk about something happening in a year or two
- Thinks you are most beautiful when you are wearing no make-up.

Take a look at **IDEA 46, *Falling too fast*, to make sure you are feeling the right things for the right reasons.**

Try another idea…

If someone says things like 'I think I'm falling for you' or 'I love the way you do that', they are making a soft space for your major 'L' word to land. If they are the kind of person for whom ordering a drink is stressful, then maybe they will feel overwhelmed and expect you to produce a ring as soon as you say it; don't expect someone to be up to your speed. If you don't know someone well enough to gauge whether or not saying 'I love you' is their equivalent of picking baby names then you probably aren't ready to move to that stage anyway.

'If you have built castles in the air, your work need not be lost, that is where they should be. Now put foundations under them.'
HENRY DAVID THOREAU

Defining idea…

Don't say it if you are feeling needy or unsure about how they feel. If they don't reciprocate (yet) they could think you are a stalker, and if they do, you could find yourself having taken things to a level you didn't intend when, frankly, you were just fishing. Be prepared for a silence, laugh or amazement; just be proud of being open and wait – easy to say but so hard to do! But this is not tit for tat; the only 'I love you' worth having is one given freely. Try and take the pressure off you both.

How did it go?

Q   Agghh! I totally got it all wrong! I blurted it out and now he hasn't called. What do I do?

A   OK. Were you having sex?

Q   Oh, why pretend I have any dignity, yes we were. So?

A   Fine; send him an email or give him a call and make a joke of it; admit you are embarrassed and then say 'I meant to say I loved that orgasm!' The added layer of flattery will help ease the path back to normality.

Q   What if he doesn't want to see me again?

A   Good riddance; we've all made a few slips of the tongue at times and if he can't cut you some slack and make you feel less embarrassed he's not right for you anyway. Move on.

The end...

Or is it a new beginning?

We hope that the ideas in this book will have inspired you to get out there and find
your Prince Charming. We hope that you've enjoyed trying out different kinds of
dates from speed dating and blind dates to holiday flings and office romances. Even if
you haven't found 'the one' yet we hope you've gained confidence and had some fun.

So why not let us know all about it? Tell us how you got on. What did it for you –
what really turned you into the queen of the dating scene? Maybe you've got some
tips of your own you want to share (see next page if so). And if you liked this book
you may find we have even more brilliant ideas that could change other areas of
your life for the better.

You'll find the Infinite Ideas crew waiting for you online at www.infideas.com.

Or if you prefer to write, then send your letters to:
Master dating
The Infinite Ideas Company Ltd
36 St Giles, Oxford OX1 3LD, United Kingdom

We want to know what you think, because we're all working on making our lives
better too. Give us your feedback and you could win a copy of another *52 Brilliant
Ideas* book of your choice. Or maybe get a crack at writing your own.

Good luck. Be brilliant.

Offer one

CASH IN YOUR IDEAS

We hope you enjoy this book. We hope it inspires, amuses, educates and entertains you. But we don't assume that you're a novice, or that this is the first book that you've bought on the subject. You've got ideas of your own. Maybe our author has missed an idea that you use successfully. If so, why not send it to yourauthormissedatrick@infideas.com, and if we like it we'll post it on our bulletin board. Better still, if your idea makes it into print we'll send you four books of your choice or the cash equivalent. You'll be fully credited so that everyone knows you've had another Brilliant Idea.

Offer two

HOW COULD YOU REFUSE?

Amazing discounts on bulk quantities of Infinite Ideas books are available to corporations, professional associations and other organisations.

For details call us on:
+44 (0)1865 514888
Fax: +44 (0)1865 514777
or e-mail: info@infideas.com

235

Where it's at...

Even more brilliant ideas...

Look gorgeous always
Linda Bird

"Looking beautiful is about much more than possessing fantastic cheek-bones and endless legs, though of course, great genes do help. The good news is that vitality, confidence, a savvy wardrobe, a few great make up and grooming tricks can work wonders too."

"Look gorgeous always will help you unlock the ravishing creature that lies within. It provides lots of simple but ingenious tips that I've learned from the leading lights in health and beauty. Try these brilliant ideas today – and feel more gorgeous, instantly!" – **Linda Bird**

Available from all good bookshops or call us on + 44 (0) 1865 514888

Perfect weddings
Lisa Helmanis

"Your wedding day. It should be the happiest day of your life, but the build-up to the big day can be so fraught with issues and anxiety that by the time it arrives you're dead on your feet and feeling stressed out."

"And then there are the problems at the reception ... how to stop your cousin Peter getting off his face at the free bar and playing air guitar to Status Quo, and how to cope with Aunty Alice and Uncle Tom re-enacting their bitter divorce of years ago while you're trying to cut the cake."

"Making it the best day of your life is all in the planning. If you follow my insider tips, whether you're getting married in a cathedral or the local registry office, you can make it a perfect day that not only you but all your guests will remember fondly forever." – **Lisa Helmanis**

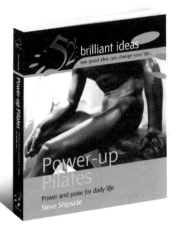

Power-up pilates

Steve Shipside

"Watered down yoga certainly had no place in my rigorous, self-disciplined programme for total fitness. But then I got the bug when I was introduced to Pilates by my physio after I had damaged my back. It's a total work-out for body and mind, and now I'm fitter, more flexible and more relaxed than I ever dreamed I could be. I just had an idea that I could make it work for me and then worked out how. Then I did it. Now I have developed a unique programme to help others get more out of their Pilates sessions." – **Steve Shipside**

Available from all good bookshops or call us on + 44 (0) 1865 514888

Cultivate a cool career

Ken Langdon

"My career had started so well. I was going places in a go-ahead business. I had a boss who thought I was wonderful and the future looked fantastic. It all changed when our company was bought out. My old boss left and if my new boss had had one more brain cell he'd have been a half wit. I was in danger of going from bright young thing to old has-been in a matter of months. Then it struck me – couldn't I devise a series of strategies to help me jump-start my career? That's what I did – I took responsibility, boosted my earnings and, just as important, started enjoying work again. If I can do it, so can you, especially as this book contains all the ideas that helped me succeed." – **Ken Langdon**